O Resplandor

O Resplandor

ERÍN MOURE

ANANSI

This edition published in 2010 by
House of Anansi Press Inc.
110 Spadina Avenue, Suite 801
Toronto, ON, M5V 2K4
Tel. 416-363-4343
Fax 416-363-1017
www.anansi.ca

Distributed in Canada by
HarperCollins Canada Ltd.
1995 Markham Road
Scarborough, ON, M1B 5M8
Toll free tel. 1-800-387-0117

Distributed in the United States by
Publishers Group West
1700 Fourth Street
Berkeley, CA 94710
Toll free tel. 1-800-788-3123

House of Anansi Press is committed to protecting our natural environment. As part of our efforts, this book is printed on paper that contains 100% post-consumer recycled fibres, is acid-free, and is processed chlorine-free.

14 13 12 11 10   1 2 3 4 5

Library and Archives Canada Cataloguing in Publication

Moure, Erín, 1955–
O resplandor / Erín Moure.

Poems.
ISBN 978-0-88784-814-8

I. Title.

PS8576.O96O34 2010   C811'.54   C2009-905628-3

Library of Congress Control Number: 2009936541

Text design and typesetting: Sari Naworynski

Canada Council   Conseil des Arts   ONTARIO ARTS COUNCIL
for the Arts   du Canada   CONSEIL DES ARTS DE L'ONTARIO

We acknowledge for their financial support of our publishing program the Canada Council for the Arts, the Ontario Arts Council, and the Government of Canada through the Canada Book Fund.

Printed and bound in Canada

Contents

El amor se produce cuando se acaricia una textura, cuando con las manos, o con la boca, se relata. La boca acaricia con relatos, provoca texturas aquí y allá. Y en las texturas se puede leer. Pero casi nadie sabe leer.

Ana Becciú, *Ronda de Noche*

PART ONE

The Nichita Stănescu Translations by Elisa Sampedrín

—•—

We must give up trying to know those to whom
we are linked by something essential: by this I mean we must
greet them in the relation with the unknown in which
they greet us as well, in our estrangement.

— Maurice Blanchot, *Friendship*

from **Initial Elegy**

cos dedos estendidos, tócote . . .

It's not the love of no one
but that no-one had yet penetrated
the air of anyone daring far off
to face fully the air's possible loveliness.

Air's loveliness crowns her, and i am made to know
this, though it is something i so rarely know,

unless . . .

Non é o amor de ninguén
senón que nin-quén xa penetrara
o aire de al-guén atrevendo de lonxe
a encarar completamente a posíbel fermosura do aire

CRÓNICA ONE
Elisa Sampedrín:

I stood before the screen of my own language. There was no remedy. Either I stood before the original work in its incredible beauty or I stood before the screen of my own language. Before this screen, I had no recourse. Something had to be altered in my body, to compensate for the screen of my language that stood between me and the poem. I unsocked myself. I unshoed myself.

I was a stalk of grain and light.

—

I was alone in Bucureşti. In its traffic. An absolute clamorous din. I had to change my face.

—.

When I first started translating Stănescu, I didn't know Romanian. "Albă" looked to me like "albumin," so I translated it as albumin. Later I found out it was the feminine of "white." Albumin then became even more accurate. Stănescu was urgently saying *albumin*.

My mouth filled up utterly with this word.

Something the same happened with all the others. Bucureşti. Why did I go there.

(after Chus Pato)

— Do you know this is the ruin of translation if you go on like this?
— . . .

·4

— You only discover what is bad and foul about literature, don't you?

— . . .

— And not only that . . .

— . . .

—

I can't explain why I was so suddenly drawn to translation. But surely it was the poems of Stănescu. In Bucureşti, in a bookstore, or in the street, the din. Or I was standing in a hallway, someone's hall (whose?) and slid the book off a shelf. It had such a worn cover, pale yellow. I intended to put it back the instant that feet sounded in the corridor. But when I gently opened the book, I saw cattle. An eyeful of cattle. Their field was steaming. It was after a rain. A man was hammering on a stone. He wasn't watching me at all, he was so intent. I heard feet then. The book slipped into my coat. One gesture. But my mouth hurt. I raised my eyes then and took the book out, and held it to the waiting woman. She turned to the shelf, then back to me without saying anything. I knew I had to translate it. I knew no Romanian. But I wanted to read the book, so I had to translate it.

There would be no surcease until I did so.

Erín Moure:

I'd been reading translations all day, O.A.'s unpublished ones of Paul Celan from Romanian to English, translations that occurred in the space between poems, and . . . true, the line was not there. But when I looked up, I had said it out loud. The line had formed itself in my mouth and I heard it spoken. What had I translated? I opened the window. How could I have translated something into English that was already in my own tongue? The echo of vehicles on stone walls. It was Celan. Early Celan. *There is an essential anachrony in our being exposed to the other at the moment of translation,* said Derrida (or not). "Contagious fire and hours that break all clocks."

—

Each time, time's rupture must be admitted, for every translation destroys time. This is not "an impossible sentence with no meaning." It is the time or tense of all translation, all writing. Like the future anterior of the phrase "I died," all translation appears as a monster in time itself.

—

"I told myself the following, which I feel with singular acuteness and intensity: if this interiorization is not possible, if it cannot — and this is the unbearable paradox of fidelity — be completed, it would not be because of a limit, a border that cannot be crossed, a frontier that encloses a given space, organizing finitude into an inside and outside homogeneous with one another, symmetrical and commensurable. It would be, rather, because of another organization of space and of visibility, of the gazing and the gazed upon." (Jacques Derrida, *Work on Mourning,* words underlined by E.S. in a book slipped into the library of E.M. by the window, beside bpNichol's *Translating Translating Apollinaire.*)

E.S.:

How did I first encounter Stănescu? The story of the book in the Bucureşti hallway, it is true, never happened. Or it happened much later. Or it had happened years before, to someone else, who told it to me that evening last spring. We were on the roof terrace in the low wooden chairs, just gazing upward into dusk, not talking. Swallows soared out from the church eaves into the late blue vault of the sky.

—

They say there are non-image-forming photoreceptors in the ganglion cells of the retina that in receiving light produce not images but our sense of time. Circadian rhythm. Cells most sensitive to the blue range of the visible spectrum. Thus they looked at the impact of blue light on the structure of sleep. By exposing subjects to blue light in the evening, not letting them shift posture. Now sleep is blue-shifted, they say. We see more and more blue. While the non-image-forming receptors alter our absorption of time. They call it a "circadian phase delay." It seems that time itself is detained by blue light.

(fallen from a notebook in Elisa's hotel room in Bucureşti, and caught on the heel of a shoe . . . found later in the hallway under a buzzing fluorescent lamp)

—

When I first picked up O.A.'s book of Stănescu's poetry, I realized that not only did it give me access to the poems in my second language, English, it gave me access to the original, Romanian. At this point I ceased to understand any language. I had to translate it, in order to read again. Yes, it was already translated beautifully,

7

but the translator had given me an original too. This shocked me. It was in a language I could not read and it entered me. I could not turn away from it.

—

Past the fiery red signal of Betelgeuse and down into the realm of the sky's diamond, Sirius. Out there in the constellation Orion. "Talk instead about the line of expressiveness." I folded in the ink of the sky above us on the roof that day.

—

And further, we don't even need the retina at all. "We developed a non-invasive method to measure human clock gene expression in oral mucosa and show how this gene oscillates. We already had the first evidence that induction of *PER2* expression is stimulated by exposing subjects to 2 hours of light in the evening. The non-image-forming visual system is already demonstrably involved in human circadian gene expression. Now we also know there is a functional circadian machinery in human buccal samples."

The mouth itself responds to light. We feel time passing, this way, in the mouth.

Inheritance

Father my father died of dying
undied himself from my mother
even from me his daughter, he unlocked his shoulder-case
and self-undied.

My father died snowing
or not even snowing yet, unsuspecting the place
where his lungs existed.

He got up and said
"it appears to be snowing," lucent with orchids you can
hardly see.

From that height he saw snow and
i saw his chair empty, his big chair, up above
it was empty,
the chair he always wore.

Even when he was smaller, he wore it,
even when he still knew his mother, he wore it
he wore and wore the chair
he had climbed up into it when his father had died
and he wore it

and this
and that
and orchids.

And my son came home astonished
or tired,
and climbed into the chair, and sighed.

Trying to Contact a Ghost

No more on this trip will the wall bow down to me
kindly.
No more a beard of earth stilled in the hand's palm.
No more blood and pain, bowed to me,
inimically mine, i fear.
Aerial in the heights, when you are heightened
my tryst's sadness is heightened.
Time comes back, when death falls.
Time comes forward, intimate as a machine.
Time comes still, when the plough is
about to cut again,

and every familiar comes wearing your cap
over the rocky trail.
The mare passes and comes, touching the plough,
showing her teeth, pale as albumin.

It Came at 5 p.m.

After ploughing so far off, their hoofs are steaming.
So i admit it: nature is life, it's not dead after all.
I give you my intelligence
and plunge into salty tears
before whetting the chalk
lifted up by the plough:
no, i'm not depraved
i'm grieving, i'm grieving, i'm grieving
the yoke-beam of cattle worn as fate,
necrotizing care in my eyes,
infradragonal, if you can taste it.
My sentimentality is no stunt, but the discretion of cattle
and, thanks to her
my flesh is flesh and that's all.
It's my flesh. That's all.
Their hooves are hot and wet, and their sides
are breathing.

Pietà

Die Welt ist fort, ich muss dich tragen. Paul Celan

This pietà
is a man
in the care of another man
as tomorrow begs them
into the most gentle
torsion of a foot in the back

this back, in turn, touches the foot
back, gently

!flesruoy fo erac ekaT

Requiem for a Mountain Climb

There's such smudged light up here
smudged limit of the sky
right to the sea the limit plunges.
It's like eight people feeling pain,
and rice being thrown over their shoulders,
spraining something
gaining wings
that the rest of us are deprived of,
so close and so far, scared and tripling
with oats and cattle.
Let's go early from here,
really, let's get going.
Scared become cattle
and the oats curl.

On my way down
i'll climb a stepladder
and i'll be cured!

Defrocked Ending

Tomorrow's hand-locked.
Nothing can uncurl its fingers.
Artful
or touching on artful, it is a suit unworn
as if the suit in itself, hung up and artful
could jab outward and deliver me a punch.
Nothing about scandal.
It's a suit in itself unworn
about to unhang itself and
deliver me a punch.
Nothing gives priority to such a meeting.
Nothing soars, no stars, no moon.
Everything's a mimic.
As such, it's gone punchy. And i'm aching
or loquacious,
veering closer, mug up, leaning into the punch.

CRÓNICA TWO
E.S.:

I walk to bed each night in a blur, leaving my glasses where they'll be close to my work in the morning. It is as if my eyes do not want to leave language. I can only work here, or in the field.

The field is behind a textile factory, or what had been a textile factory, now it is a factory of textiles, small companies occupying the structure and making what they please. All that remains of unity is the huge name on the side which declares, in typical Eastern fashion, grandiose: "Paris Star." The language of no one appropriated perfectly, in a land where no one speaks it. The field is grassy, dry though, full of broken bits of foundation and rail ballast. The rails are long gone, the ties taken up and used elsewhere.

—

I dreamed it once. I've already said that. It disturbed me. It was as if I wanted him to put his language directly into my mouth. But there is a line that can or cannot be crossed in translation. I didn't want to cross it. I tried not to. It's not language of course. But what's attached to language. Its carbuncle. The body. I went out into the road, into the deafening din of tramcars, automobiles, doors shutting, shoes scraping and voices. I swore I would never cross it.

—

I soon realized my approach was not the right one. I just had to read his poems, the way they were. The way I was able to receive them. That way the language would be transferred directly inside me. Through the hands and eyes. It is really the hands and eyes then. The face, still, and the palm. The mouth is always lost from the beginning. *As my mouth was lost to me the moment it found . . .*

—

Yet I could not shake the cattle, his cattle, out of my mind. The herd bunched up, their warm backs and shoulders, a material and organic *existenza* in the world that the poem co-enacted, undressed, unfaced. These cattle were as urgent to me as thought itself. I had to keep returning there. *Gando. Gânduri.*

—

I went out into the field and looked at my hands. Today they are hurting. The old ache I inherited, from my mother. There is a space between each finger and it is full of grasses, gravel, bits of old plastic. So that I see the world through the fingers of the hands. I felt safe then. But anxious. Was I trying to wish him alive again? Sometimes I think that what I had was so contagious that such monstrosity was . . . *[grass-smudged and not finished]*
. . .

. . .

—

In the dirt behind the factory, I unhanded myself. In the field with its blades of herb and crickets, with its blackbirds crackling in the derelict cedar, I unhanded myself. I unhanded myself of the old, old residue. The residue touched my palm. I unhanded myself then. I unpalmed myself. My cocked wrists drove my hands numb entirely. I uncocked them. I untriggered the wristbone. The socket opened and the tiny blade. I unheld my hand.

E.M.:

It was O., the woman on the roof, who first showed me that photo. I photocopied it to have one for myself. She had been carrying it for a year, when I first spoke to her. She'd taken it in Bucharest, or what I called Bucharest, and O. called București. Elisa called it București too. When O. said she took the photo, I thought she'd held the camera, and was utterly startled, but it turned out she'd taken it in a different way. It had been left in a book in the library where O. had been working on her translations of Nichita Stănescu, or so she said. It didn't belong to the library, clearly, and O. felt it was hers, and took it. She wasn't sure who it depicted. I was able to confirm it was Sampedrín.

—

I can only think about some things in the field, my field, the one with no name at all in the east of Montreal. The textile mills here still hammer away; they have no air conditioning and their windows are flung open in summer and I hear them pounding and hissing. Cloth is a byproduct of this noise. What do I think about? The incommensurate. How could O. find a photo of Elisa Sampedrín in Bucharest while translating Stănescu, when E.S. first discovered Stănescu in the very translations O.A. had made into English? It was those translations that had spurred E. to vanish in Bucharest. But O., when I met her, had had Sampedrín's photograph for months. And now I have a photocopy of the photograph, in the field, in this fabric of heat and noise.

—

Dear O.: Never let me meet Elisa. Never let me ask her to put language into my mouth. E.
Dear E.: You can't meet Elisa now, don't worry. She's not there.

That was a year ago at least, when I was translating Stănescu in București. Or before that. So it's already past. Don't worry. O.

—

At the same time I realized I'd seen something in the photo of Elisa that I couldn't tell O. about.

It was one of the women walking in the background, getting off the white tram in Bucharest. She had been looking at E. with a kind of astonishment. As if about to ask her something. E. didn't see her at all. This was clear. And in the photo, of course, the woman had already looked away, into the air. It troubled me for weeks, ever since O. showed me E.'s image. I felt I needed to go to Bucharest. But I couldn't leave. It agitated me so much, until I realized that Montreal would have to be Bucharest now. Later I could correct it. So I had to find O. again. To ask her to rename my street for me, or rename a few critical streets. The rest didn't matter. Which Bucharest streets would my own streets be? What were their equivalents? I had to find her.

rue Henri-Julien =
rue Rachel =
rue = . . .

Anatomy Lesson

In the middle of my spread palm
so perfumed
i know you will see me unfaced
if i raise my hand, such a sunflower.

I take off my shirt before dinner
i take off my socks
i know you will see me unfaced
if i tremble
if impudent i turn my head
and pull my blanket off the blanket
like tomorrow
beside a brook, wings broken off
i know you will see me unfaced
if i leave behind my blanket like a burka.
I ask you please for more tumult
and take my disguise seriously, up to my lips
convincingly,
no palace entering your furor.
I'm not an iron statue
i'm perfumed
perfumed like a doorway,
if my imbrication cures me,
luminescent sunlight, if you please.

Self-Portrait

I was never as tall as you imagined.
My drop of blood
fell from a word.

Self-Portent

It's a tall order.
A raspberry crushes my hand
too. Some blood flows out,
some tries to get in.

Self-Portrayal

I had never felt all visible.
A patch of blood,
a face, a word.

Selfish Portrait

A bird in the rowan last winter.
I lowered my eyes
a moment, i was not animal.
The red clutch of berries, and me looking,
my skin pried upward.
I could not face a bird.

Living Proof

And so, i took the temperature of the mouth.
And so, i took the temperature of the armpit.
Washing it first, patting it dry, closing
the arm to the body,
tucking the elbow where the waist is.

And so, i took the temperature of the anus,
bending my arm around my back
to do so.

Churchbells rang out, it was noon.
No-one was outside on the road.

Everywhere, everywhere, everywhere:
the same temperature.

(a translation with no original)

22

Leaving the Battalion

— With what acumen do you visualize, the horse asked
the sleeping soldier.
— Uncle, uncle, uncle uncle,
uncle, uncle, uncle, uncle.
Acumen of the sleeping soldier, visualizing
when he dreamed, with copious outcry,
aspirated, his copious outcry
when he visualizes uncle.
An uncle he can't see, uncle of which
of which of which
— When you visualized so copiously, what did you feel?
— I never saw or felt anything,
i said uncle, uncle, uncle, uncle,
uncle.
— If it was so copious,
why did you dream uncle, and call out?
— I never dreamed uncle, i said
uncle, uncle, uncle, uncle.
— Uncle, so copious?
— Uncle.
— A simple call, copious.
— Uncle.

Grief's Door

What if a stone fell bright in my fingers,
under night's tarpaulin, with the cattle resting
and with the stone i was golden
and incongruous, pregnant with the stone's face
animating my sobs
and forbidding me smooth sleep?

Yet i sleep with the grandeur of cattle every day
sewing used clothes
that were torn when the stone fell.
Yet in my sleeping, a cataract may come to roar
with its forehead alternating spray,
with a shoulder captured alternating sore

so that those asleep at the foot of the roar
their tremulous vision altered by the roar
the face of their vision altered by the roar

where they lay, just as a wet trout leaps out of spray,
while i sleep in the tent with knees up to chin
sewing used clothing with the eye beam fallen from stone.

Dictate

By its wheated thread, it penetrated
worked tin, my lips' opening.
By its parasite, it penetrated
deeply my pectoral cloud, to merge with
sky.
By its singular anchor, it penetrated
bleeding me of verse in the sea's
oration.
And so. All coasts arrive
at this barrier.
And light spreads. Imprudently, the melee
in the body raises its unique mask.
For here i did not exist yet,
wings open, and so, and so, this.

(a very *brief history of translation)*

Evocation

As beautiful as the idea of a shoulder,
the skin of a cup that mirrors the spine,
the spartan stone confesses
stubbornly in the dead limb.
It was not milled oats, it breathed.
It rubbed and pleaded with the sea's tears
it was serrated and sandy
glad levity inviting the barbarian stranger.

It was beautiful as the shoulder of cattle,
between the grass and flies,
between the light of August as dreamed in April
and, and, it was only the palm of her hand.

Splay with a Stone

Create voice with bone,
tip voice with steel,
die voice with a journey,
clot voice with a word
and you, unconditionally
Plough with a stone from the pyramids
plough with a stone
and don't splay the earth, and don't splay
it, gather singular
singular
Without make-believe,
without making time.

Cold Fulguration

All of this said short and dated,
insistent, presence simply ripened.
Such lucre trampled into light doubly-amazed,
yearly,
looped to a cord, the wings of evening
make their foam in another higher cavern,
such wings of evening, evening of evening.
I am simply present for a history of ripening
printed black, printed, in short,
with discretion, captured in rapture,
its odour of a photograph of the sea without suffering.
In this way, captured doubly with a branch of flowers,
of family, printed with a feminine tulip
doubly lost and visibly wilting
denied the shore of another diurnal turn in time
this verb in the ear of a further cavern,
presence ripened in history and in historical.
From the radius of its pulse my depth is stronger,
with the pomp of a ripening that curtails explosions
yet multiplies basically the discretion of prayer
gone electric in the mouth's entrance, this ripening
utterly nocturnal,
with acumen, doubling my year of exile.
Its placenta is the guts of the house, where the patient first entered.
I am simply brusque, spinal,
rushing forward, orbiting in layers
yes, fulgurating, twisting the chipped house of the sprained body,
oh you cold, you fulguration!
Ingenious this bitter odour i married,
bitter this sea tied to the frame of my open window.
Odour of the east that mocks me.
Fulgurant, still.

Human Pain

If i put my foot down on this fact, a blanket fact
the light of a blanket in my hand, a cloth in my hand
a face, ridicule's blanket.
And someone looks back at the human form
cloth when all becomes fruitful
leaning all bent before a plate of venison
behaving, thankfully, like a treble fact.
You can give my poet's pain to that man's fibre
a state of pain caught up painful in the sheet of the man
so naked the threads are torn loose from him.
Give it here, man,
boldly, as a professional of boldness.
You can't make it come back by praying or pretend,
and if this thread were sewn up all over?

A shroud, a shroud, wet ground empty of children,
nighttime, a wet field,

empty, a shroud, a shroud.

The photo arrived under my door in Montreal. Like an advertising flyer but this was definitely no advertisement. The woman in the photo had her head turned away. She was walking out of the camera frame very fast to the left, wearing stockings and trousers at once. With three hands. Not looking at me. I blurted out: *Elisa.* The blue of her bag was the same blue as the balconies on the building behind her. Squat, concrete, residential. A random heap of gravel at its side, a bit of grass, a chunk of yanked-up concrete. A tree gone to ruin. Laundry. Elisa. Bucharest, some outskirt, one of those inner city outskirts, it could only be. I could almost smell cooking from an open window, and Elisa had groceries. In a plastic bag. In full stride. Her tall figure making a perfect A. Already leaving the frame.

Then I realized. Elisa can't have three hands. And more disturbingly: I knew the third hand. It was pointing outward to the left of the photo, an address or convocation. Bringing something into the clear. I'd definitely seen that hand before. On the roof terrace in the wind that afternoon in Montreal, resting on the arm of a wooden chair. It was O.'s hand.

I didn't know what to think.

I almost panicked.

—

: O. had found the photo of Elisa in the book in the library a year after it was left there, when she was first translating Stănescu and doing research in Bucharest.
: Elisa had gone to București to find Stănescu, as a result of reading

O.'s translations of his poems in a bookstore on Bank Street in Ottawa; the translations had been made, by then, several years before, and published at least a year earlier.

—

I couldn't get around it. O. knew E.S. Not only that, but likely she had cooked and eaten a meal with E.S. in a concrete outskirt of Bucharest. Nowhere near a library. And who is that figure watching them both from the balcony? That third hand, O.'s hand, penetrates the photo, though O. is nearly completely obscured by the striding Elisa. I look down at my own hands, opening them. I will have to go back up on the roof, and see her hand again, just to make sure. I have to find O.

(Handscrawled in E.M.'s notebook, then torn out. Days later, it blew into the street as the blue bin was upturned into the recycling truck. A woman, passing, picked it up in one hand as she walked by. She read the first few lines and broke out laughing. O.)

— —

But O. had told me not to worry, that Elisa had last been seen years before O.'s own translations of Stănescu. That she was gone. All she had of E.S. was the photo, and she hadn't even known at first who it depicted. It was me who told her it was Elisa Sampedrín.

It came to me that O. was somehow withholding something from me.

—

Dear O. I don't know if this note will reach you. Could we meet again? I have a few questions to ask you for my research. Not urgent, really. But could we meet? We could go sit on the roof again, if you liked. Please call if you get this. E.

Dear E. I am out of town awhile. I could send someone else who could help you, perhaps even better than I can. O.

—

When my mouth hurts, I know I have done it. My mouth hurts down into my chest, the lung aches, it is my mouth hurting even there. It hurts in the centre of my palms. I translate Celan and feel myself all aching mouth everywhere. And I translate him accurately, for I translate him from English, a language I can read without difficulties. Though perhaps, properly speaking, it is O.A. whom I am translating. For it is her who gives me this tremulous Celan from his *limba română* into the language of my own emptiness, *engleză*. I have to trust her. To do my own translations at all, I have to trust her.

—

Dear O. Please, no. Not that. I'll wait for you to come back from your trip. E.

—

O.'s postcard arrived today. Postmarked two weeks ago already. A photograph from Călărași where she was born. People outside a department store that seemed to be called Muntenia. I scanned their immobile figures with the magnifier. None of them were Elisa. I felt relieved. On the back of the card, just a few looped words:

= Strada Matei Voievod

= Strada Austrului
= Stradă.   O.

—

Then I saw O. had also penned an X on the face of the photo, marking the seventh floor of a building further down the street. X. Language signing its own signature. I was beginning to feel that ache in my mouth again. I put the postcard in a drawer, hurriedly, and leaned out the casement. The sun bled around the corners of the building and refracted, half blinding me. Matei Voievod was an utter clamour of sirens and traffic. A fire engine was trying to turn into the narrow street, blocked by a parked car, which the sappers were now trying to push onto the sidewalk. I pulled my head in. My face hurt so. I remembered what Elisa had written to Chus, so long ago, when E. was in Tokyo studying kabuki. *"For you, always, i don my disguise, ashen."* Suddenly I understood what she was saying. For I felt like that now, about O.

—

". . . the thought of the *virtual work* . . . that would accomplish the possible *as such* without effacing it or even enacting it in reality. The thought of a spectral power of the virtual work . . . Only death, which is not, or rather mourning, which takes its place in advance, can open up this space of absolute *dynamis*: the possible as such." (Jacques Derrida, *Work on Mourning*)

—

"We constantly, giddyingly, mangle each other's languages, but in mangling them we enter them, we see each other fully, we acknowledge and thus open the possible, entirely, *as such*."

(from a notebook of O.'s, left at E.M.'s, possibly by accident)

I knew O. was not writing about me, but about E.S. I felt the terrifying plunge of an elevator. As if my endocrine system were reeling to a stop.

—

Dear E. I'm back in B. from C. It's great to hear you are on M.V. Could meet you tomorrow before I fly back to Montreal? I think I left a notebook in your apartment last time, at least, I can't find it in my bags here. Oh, and you're not quite right that the letter is the smallest unit of translation. O.

Dear O.
~~Dear O.~~
O.

—

I couldn't write her the message at all. It wouldn't speak. I was given over to language and it was withholding itself even from me. I'd seen the third photo by then, not on paper but in an email that had landed in my spam box. It was of a woman in summer dress, sleeveless, about my own age probably, holding a rope attached to a low wagon of sorts, a slab of plywood on wheels, really, laden with boxes and a huge wrapped bag. She was stopped in the road among the cars. There were two people on a stoop as well, not looking at her, young women outside an apartment block. And a figure on the balcony above. Who?

At the far left edge of the photo, walking off into the distance, carrying what looked like a small sofa between them, were two other women. The photographer had caught O. and E.S. entirely by accident. But I recognized O.'s blue bag. And E.'s walk, even though she was immobile in the photograph, and had her back to me.

I shut the computer.

⁓

"This *being-to-for* obliges us to think the image not as reproduction of what it would imitate, not as *mimeme* . . . but as the increase of power, the origin, in truth, of authority, the image itself becoming the author, the author and the augmentation of *auctoritas* insofar as it finds its paradigm, its *enargeia*, in the image of the one who has been lost, in the one about to be mourned." (J.D., *altered by E.M.*)

Dear Valentine

Valentine, thou, feigned citizen
face me with the lost imperative
face gently my non soil
lay down in my plain soil
plough the fortunate sea
past the Black Sea, seaward
Valentine
Valentine
Valentine
Valentine
Is this poem even sadder
than my country of origin,
your name?

My Fear

My fear of lightning in the face, unintelligible
my fear of nodding faces won't dislodge
my fear of cattle, my fear of wafers
of flack and favours
My smell gone cold and yours at most
that leaves me fearing my own ghost
dislodging cranes from each wet field
In time this temper yields
to a stirring in the blood
as i stretch out, old, limping
shaking a bit, get on, i'm not going to be born
as anyone's twin, it wouldn't be prudent
Me shaking with words, and my mother so ill,
kind star i lean on, whose root bends to me.

Libelous Stain

Hands penetrate to the second verse
and with dark eyes libelous
penetrate right to the random apex
transparent
penetrate to the farcical ignominious boar
penetrate to the staid moviehouse where facts become
facultative
penetrate the sumptuous and suave sun
penetrate the stick of the sweetest sun
penetrate where no words have yet penetrated
nor sun convoked nor verb or word.
Libelous hands penetrate in my emptied place
tasting gold
penetrate in the sun's vital aura
penetrate the good fact.

Libelous hands penetrate the intelligent leg,
the hand penetrates with the contemporary sun, hers,
the hand penetrates until it intercepts another hand
the sweet smell of your hand in my hand
as if it were infinitely more grotesque.
The hand penetrates until it is uncertain
if it still a limb,
a real limb of flesh
so imbricated in the void
that it leaps, coveting
a third stanza, coveting dark-bright eyes,
apart from mine, hungering.

To My Breath's Psyche

One day it came to me suddenly:
— I'll fall down like a pig,
a jig-parody of a rat.
Put grass under the shadow of my face to quiet it;
then wait to see if i'm still breathing!
— From this, i'm stricken, from this?
— Watch yourself!
One day it came suddenly to me:
— She's a stickler for travesty
even with my stubborn thoughts opened to hers!
And before i am cured and die like a worm
i wear my forefoot in nary a boot, in a rat, in a trumpet!
— In this, i'm stricken, in this?
— Watch yourself! I once was an engineer . . .
Apex of an engineer, ah, engineer, ah, engineer, ah, engineer
pleats in her skirts and an excitable air
in the airless air of the air.
Flute of the air
trilling an aura of engineer of the air.
Too excitable by far,
she's engineered all the air, all of it!
You'll leave at four when the air leaves,
in the sunny face, agile, of the air?
— And can't i leave with you, i'm stricken
from this wound in the bronchials, from this?
— Watch yourself, the air rasped, watch yourself . . .

How to Get Out of the Army

only to ignite, in memory Tomasz Grędysz

The incipient General
called Emperor in the official tongue
or, up close, Captain
in the vernacular tongue of footsoldiers
duped in ranks and parading past
duped ranks and parading past
meadows of oxen uncorded and gnawing rank grass:

Timbre, his, generally, his barbaric insufflation
duped timbre, captainic, his barbaric insufflation
insist: barbarians
duped barbarians, barbed
duped barbary, plodded
duped plodders, played out
duped players, hooting
duped hoots, illusory illusion in their timbre while
words — *run!* — to the forest with belches, in boots.

Part-Elegy

the roof between visceral and real

What comes from afar,
sent half-late and chilled
rosy as dawn to my singularity.
In cathedrals with pulse perceptible, half-late,
swirling and absorbing the intrusion of belief,
in an absurd circuit
right in the zone of absurdity,
raying with the sea drunk with moonlight,
in the gold of what exists.
The cinders of fury, nightly,
luminous eyes sleeping,
innumerous dints glow in the face taken up with sleep
sharing the tunic
seeding a plot of meteors
on the street of light called *strada luminată*
urging and corroborating together.
What comes from afar,
sent half-late to me
and
my own properties now are too naked
and much more intelligent
my own properties too are enraged
by a poet who exists and is leaving
too, enraged.
Astral,
grabbing the last step of the insomniac stair
in the evening of evening,
yearning
in the partial but unconjugated
strata of ice,
courting discards and

scuffling with insufficiency,
vale
of my care and my possibility of freedom
unnegotiable
with its possibility that all of this is a film, and over.

II

To be all bothered in myself with this rupture,
accepting
its rigours hugely, attuned to the procession
that seems will endure.

Endure and rupture in the gift of light,
the pattern it prints on my eyes, aches.
Endure and rupture in soaring
light,
the sound of loving bells, ache.
Endure ruptured in ache
in the mirrored sunlight,
and what touches my nostril, ache.
And you, oh you, remaking the entire inner world,
you, possibly my twin, helping me
imbricate the barbarity of the femur, yes,
oh, you, and you, and you
inhaling solemnly
the ruptured twinship
with flames of ash, detained by ash,
the prow of your voyage lit up with my fire
enrapts me,
teaches me rigour, accepting,
professing, throwing me into the lifeboat,
teaching me rigour, over and over, to climb up again
rugged, unold.

Geometrical Transport

No way i stand still.
I'm a hazard.
No way i'm a pond,
i'm a cataract
penetrating the mortiferous mortar,
penetrating the pestilent river,
penetrating the drought's stars,
penetrating white and dead incredulity
, admitting to stubbornness.
If it were only so easy. I'd be a lighthouse
at the pyramids.

I'd be a pyramid
to the stars.

Initial Elegy

half dressed with fingers outstretched, touching . . .

With cinema so far off, i am yet
incipient with film.
This, though i never dressed a Nietzschean dawn, never
pressed my arms to the tail of the comet.

In the naked strata of *far off* i saw
inimitably, in nakedness, the air chip
new forms. The air's intractable week
thus comes to me full circle,
face to face with my own cells that troop
inflagrant with dynamites torn from their own skin
potentially. To give them Nietzsche's apples to chew:
the cat's peel in a soft circle.

It's this landing, here, devoured
and
drawn far off from the margins' deep
limit:
the void doesn't gift itself to us to be seen.

Nor does the menace of history
own up to its miscarriage, such
is the coat of its seed that it co-habits gently with menace,
all credentials
fallen . . .

II

Nor are Nietzsche's apples truly present,
in desire and grain of the well's depth
with its ring of air.
It's this landing's diversity, various,
an interior punctuation yet unused, more acute
than a film's punctuality.

III

It's not the love of no one
but that no-one had yet penetrated
the air of anyone daring far off
to face fully the air's possible loveliness.

Air's loveliness crowns her, and i am made to know
this, though it is something i so rarely know,
unless . . .

IV

Here when i sleep, i conjure her.

Totalities can be inversed totally.
There are gifts so naked i cannot oppose them,
their attachment so fierce where they do not negate me:

To feel pain in the No, while
facing steadfast forward with a foot in Yes.
Beside her, facing totally steadfast her totality,
the No and the Yes are broken in the air.

So i sleep no more here,
integral and sheer with barbarity
in the face of no harbour but this port.

And how surely barbarity populates me
in the face of her shoulder. Surely as she bares
her shoulder's face.

If Nietzsche had not looked. I am
the penalty faced with the void.

Better to turn ripening and sleep —
here, yes,
in the variety of possible landings, sleep —
my face incipient with cinema
and far off from film,
having never dressed the Nietzschean dawn,
and never wanting more than now to reach out to the comet's
tail.

Doubled Elegy, Ethical

basically driven

One of us was scorched by it.

It caused even stone to crack open, repeatedly dust
entered even the sky.

We are an adjustment of the pod's rupture,
that seizes locally the seed of the sky,

here were we chosen, separately groping asphalts,
so as to seize, innately, the sky.

Oh, i never took your hand without piquancy,
when i said gracefully the said things,
i never said them for the sake of saying.

In the net of this sky our indebtedness soars,
all of it above us, as if pretending,

though in seizing the sky nearest us
we inch forward, we are penetrated by
all the sky waking up as if it were naturally ours.

So i let ache ache in me, so that i do not lose you
from my eyes, let you
penetrate my seeing so gentle so i may seize you
in orbit, as sky.
And if you won't stay, be not impervious to our we,
if you won't mix your breath with me, exalting breath . . .
If the perfume of you were to stir up breath

i would exalt, as a foot does,
strangely rising

or a seed, seizing locally the grass of the sky.

Sovereign

My torso is throne for your somnolence
ô you who reign
My word is bread dark to your longing
ô you who reign
My eyes crown you where you
reign
You make my Saturday your Sunday
and oh you reign
The time in which i lie beside you is your gift
in which i'm reined
Your sadness lets me lift the chalk of dawn sky's
rain
Your far prairie is my mortal grain
ô, you who reign.

CRÓNICA FOUR
E.S.:

From the window it's impossible to tell if what shines is footpath or *regato*. I arrived so late in Călăraşi, evening is long gone, but I've found the room and rented it, and looked out and yes, I'm looking out on the same view. I know at last I will be able to translate Stănescu alongside O. But without reading her. I'll just read the Romanian of Stănescu and write the words that occur to me as fulgurations in my own tongue. My Galego I can then translate into English in the speed it takes for a retinal flicker or an ache in the throat to reach the pen.

I don't want to sleep yet. I've been staring out the window across the field to the squat buildings on the horizon, a kind of steel plant given over to manufacturing who knows what, maybe even steel. I taste the sour yellow of the smoke, even in the dark. And between it and my room, the field, with its night clamour of dogs.

O.'s field.

The field of the translator who'd brought me here. Unwittingly. I'd not been able to find her in Bucureşti (she'd left a year ago, they said) but I've at least come to her field, and her window.

—

Footpath or water, water's footpath. Waterfoot. Grove of water.

—

To quiet my mind, I've just translated the first poem. I'm going to call it "Human Pain." That seems right. After I did it, I looked over at O.'s English, surprised. Turns out it's the title poem of her book *Occupational Sickness*. I have arrived in more ways than one, then. I can look out into the dark of her field . . . I know it's hers because I have the photograph-postcard she'd addressed to E.M., just over a year ago. It's the same field for sure. I'd filched the card out of the mail before stuffing the rest of the flyers and bills into E.'s brass mailbox in the lobby of that magnificent building on rue Rachel. She'd never miss this one card, and I needed it. It was the image of the field that grabbed me. What intrigued me and I could not figure: in the foreground of the photo, at the bottom, an ill-defined object appeared. Later examination with the magnifier showed it to be a map, partly visible, a folded map, probably resting on the windowsill. But it wasn't a map of Bucureşti.

—

I looked more closely at the map in the photo, zooming in on it, straining my eyes, pixel by pixel. What I was seeing couldn't be right at all, it made no sense. It was a map of Calgary. On a windowsill in Romania by a field. Folded backwards so that the paper curved, as if to isolate one section of the map for reference while driving. But O. had never been to Calgary. Neither of us had. Only E.M. had.

—

In the poem where O. had translated "occupational sickness" I translated "professional of boldness." It was a poem Stănescu had written about the human man, who is also a woman, a child, and a horse, for "man" is an utterly charged word in Stănescu. Man smells of earth and skin, and the clothing on man smells like skin too. Man wears a coat, or some swaddling always, and sits bowed before a plate of food, or is awakened by a horse braying. There is a tent, a blanket. Life, simply. The tent smells of skin too, and the earth of rain and chalk.

—

I'll go out and follow the creek or path tomorrow. If I can't find
O., I can at least walk where she has, whether on earth or in water.
The yellow stink of the air doesn't matter; a field is a field. My
throat is on fire, my tongue. I'll go where my mouth insists I go,
regardless of the time it takes. For the mouth itself invents time.

—

Before shutting my eyes, I read: "Friendship had thus already
come to be reflected in mourning, in the eyes of the poem, even
before friendship brought us together . . ." (Jacques D., *on Edmond
Jabès*)

—

O. is always travelling. But she's never been to Calgary. She'd
had a plan — the woman here said when I asked her about the
map this morning, offhandedly, pretending discretion — to meet
E.M. there, but that was in the future. A future that, unlike some
futures, had not yet occurred.

—

*(The walk in the field at Călăraşi is described as clouds passing across
the high vault of the sky. The text, in Galego, an old language some have
forgotten, is not reproduced here.)*

—

Instead, this: "I use these words evoking the crossroads to speak
neither of the cross where two trajectories traverse one another, or
one the other, thus assuring us that the meeting indeed took place,

nor, more literally, of the chi or the chiasm, the point of chiasm beyond which two lines lose one another to infinity. Nor do I speak of the indubitable point of tangency and contact assured by a crossing of paths. No, I am speaking of 'crossing right by one another,' from afar, without any assured contact, without any assurance, 'crossing right by one another' in an improbable 'meeting.' That is to say, without proof, forever intangible, in tangent, and intact. Without witness, the time of an interminable greeting to which each one alone and the others alone (all of them alone and each alone and without witnesses) will think they can bear witness, the 'crossing right by one another' of two at once finite and 'perpetual' arrivals, perpetually finite, having come from who knows where and from a distance that remains unascribable by anyone." (Jacques D., *on Max Loreau*)

—

When I returned from the field to the room in late morning, the map was there. It had been folded neatly along its original creases, and now lay on top of my suitcase. The windowsill was empty. I picked the map up and unfolded it. Calgary. On a small crease in the top left quadrant of the map, to the left of a large green expanse of park and beside a freeway, a circle pencilled around a word. "Watergrove." I folded the map again, feeling queasy. And returned it, decisively, to the windowsill, folded as the woman had folded it, as if it were new, not as O. had left it, folded in disarray as if distracted by driving, by the sudden need to veer left to avoid a coyote crossing the road. I carried my suitcase out of the room, paid up and said my farewell quickly to this kind woman who knew O., for I had but minutes to get to the bus station.

The Seized Elegy

unfazed sky

Stalled between two idols, i am not able
to choose, still
between two idols, hurting and ploughing the marsh,
there is no way i can choose,
stepping in air, my memory of
idols, ploughing the marsh. I stall
and have no way to choose between two
mouthfuls of mud, in ploughing a marsh what choice do i have
in this putrid rain. Stalling and
muddied, it hurts, this scraping
a white coast of earth with marsh rain.
Stalled between two furrows of chalk
i am not able to choose, stalled as Nietzsche
and ploughing the marsh, lifting earth
from the oasis of dawn, and i can't even choose.
Stalled between two grooves and ploughing the marsh
whose wings road the earth, denting it " " "_ " " " " "
with foment and sobs. " " " " " , " "
Stalled with the lopped blade of my hand, how " " " " " ,
can i choose, in the marsh rain i plough, groping doubly,
facing the void hand-first to explode it open
with a muscle of earth, lifted skyward from the marsh of rain.

" " "_ " " " " "facin gyo uhand-firs tt oexplod eu sope n

" " " " " , " "ou rmuscl eunearthe dan dchose n,seize dthreshol d

" " " " " ,fro mth emars ho frai n.

54

Scribble to the Little Man Eating Supper to the Sound of Shoes

Temples can no more
grant us space and irreversibility, little man,
so sentimentally old, faced with frost's
small feeling, feigning
and, so cautious, death's mantle
in the waves of sea and

i'll turn no more to stone in the vanity of lucre's
singularity, little man.
Come, give me that which loses itself
at the sound of shoes —
sadness, melancholy. That which
inside me loses itself
when i put on my shoes —
in the short moratorium we have from death . . .

No more supper, though its repetition each day
has value to you, little man.
Eating supper singly, eating
supper uniquely
are not values.
I turn to stone in all that light of lucre
made into value, turn to stone
and don't want even that one supper i once loved.

With an ankle sprained by the sea's acumen,
with small remains of a Grecian column, little man
of stone, that demanding material.
Its deftness, of late, potent
in the starlit passion and distraction
so artful in branches, more and higher, branches . . .

Though columns, i presume, are born in the dark frost
above such stone,
more value is incanted
in the cattle of words, little man.

It isn't much,
but better than nothing
It isn't much but it's singular,
unique and irreversible . . .

(voice lost offstage in the sound of shoes)

Tripled Elegy

when time's crimped, uncrimp it, contemplate . . .

I Contemplative Sky

As such, i triple with you,
in the cloth where we may be judged:

In which the eye divines the marks of its lauding
as a tunnel privileges
the face of one, faced with the face of the other.

And this cloth where we may be judged
privileges us; it triples:

In it we divine the marks that aid us
to unite the chafing fields we're called to face
with the blue of our carnality.

Still yet this cloth where our judgement roils us
triples blue:

In which the eye divines a foot that lauds its earth
as simply as an artery courses blood
till the face of all landscape coincides with sleep
yet sees.

II Time's Crimp

Oh, to scorch sadness, its inmost version,
your soft sigh locating a bit of meteor
apart; and in my palm i hold
rebirth in a wholly altered décor.

I throw the camera out the window, so
it can no more tear the retina of my eye.
Raising my own indigenous blue toward loam's integrity,
your eye pierces my iris.

If an amnesty from objects clothes my blood
it can't oppress me with its closeness,
and pervasive blue gives me an urge to disembark
toward the highest oration.

Oh you, who scorch sadness, you bring us
yet higher, with an oath that fills the sphere of emptiness!
Staunch in its centre, the one captivates the one,
eyes forward, eyes templed, so that our fingers

one by one by one
can descend.

III Contemplation

The air flies
as if its bird were sculpted in my spine;
she enters me by my humerus, sheerly,
occupies totality until i don't know where she stays.
In my spine's new flight to the sea
i figurate her celerity.

One hinge of her flying self touches the tarmac,
activates the planet.
Nietzsche could no more stand upright than i,
doubled over by this flowering of stone,
my hand uniting with her stalwart arms,
an arc in this apex they said did not exist.
Rivers of bird amphibians
with curled beaks agitate the heights,
my pain reverses
above sea-ink stained to black.
Rivers of birds dying,
foot facing the launch of the boat once heard
as barbarous, now migrating over the waves
to the north, lighting everywhere.

IV Crimp in Time

Could we spare ourselves a moment
from the current of this river
that slows mistily,

to give more devotion,
privileged, now yours
where your calibre can fructify it.

Surged in us, what can be?
Stopping us at no net,
engineering copiously until, here,
celerity privileges us.

Copiousness sees us, our feet now
naked as feet are.

It is as if we spare ourselves the frenzy
and the courage in it, wearing
our garland of versed eyes.

To fructify us. Hold
our heads together, privileged
in the face of succour.

V Contemporary

And if lightning strikes fire
to repeatedly flare time in the litany of her,
i stand stopped: it existed,
this vapoured dynasty of beauty Nietzsche didn't see.

Recalling in the stare of one
held in beauty, whom i loved
as properly as my own troop, with harshness,
seeing how strong i can be.

The troop lunged at me breathing into their part, up high,
until my ample embrace reached her.
I felt so global in the humerus of the east
so full of celerity and indefatigable.

Artful they accorded me my adduced lover
her light foot facing lightning intelligently,
and faced with the troop writhing
i turn to her orbit.

To no more putatively amend me.
It hurts to be tied, it taints my
foot Highvault, foot Highsnow, foot Highsky,
facing me unstintingly, to offer respite.

Gravity is mixed up in my heart,
all telluric and reclaiming
its return in full. Full with her,
i'm magnetized by these our thoughts.

Changed Elegy

a reeling attempt

I was never exceeded ever until the sea
that is sea, until the frenzy that is frenzy,
until shadow that is umber, until birds who are birds.
To be sea, frenzy, umber, bird
is to exceed me always,
and i went toward the tribunal of frenzy,
the tribunal of shadow, of sea, of bird,
a rotund tribunal, an aerial tribunal
a shuddered tribunal, i had no recourse.
I was condemned to penetrate the nest of ink,
to penetrate its folded seal, penetrate the lushness,
penetrate the mixture.
Oh, i felt you writing in a similar language.
Act of perfect accusation
with the sea-beating of wings,
and the recourse of the grey penitent, deliberate me.
I stand on my feet impecunious, my head uncovered,
circling and deciphering myself of words
penetrating ignorance,
but i can't, can't
decipher anything,
and that stare of the spirit i try to seize on,
exceeds itself in me
and condemns me, undecipherable,
to its perpetual steppingstone
to its uncorded sensibility surging in our own
cloth, in the form of sea-maker, frenzy-maker,
shadow-maker,
light-maker
bird-maker.

Sheepish Elegy

opting for the real

I carry such frenzy i'm nervous,
my green limbs galvanize and
won't perish in amnesia.
No more does stone own me, nor will i carry one last
cutting battle to the grave of stones,
but cut it repeatedly free of the machines.
It is not my place or lore
to set free symbols with their encrypted dints
but to hold and celebrate all cattle
doubly lithe in a dance of ebony.
No more will i carry the heat of misery;
with my arms' incipient mortar
and faithful hands, i embrace time
to galvanize the possible, the lore of existence.
I've never called life sacred. So much
have i seen it
accelerate in concrete form.
Having never been pristine as a star
i can't ponder
my own life.
I was in it. I carried it in the heat of day.
It dried. Pestilence retreated from it.
I carried it in the wings of birds,
and they gave me new wings to fall into the borealis.
How could i have given credence
to the void? Everything for flight.
Everything,
for the wish that lifts up the limbs of
the sky and takes flight.

So i extend my hand, and its fingers

are five hands,
thus each hand's fingers
hand five tomorrows, in which
each finger
quintuples tomorrow, in fingers.

Everything for the embrace!
Each bit, everything,
for piping up reborn to shake off privilege,
and for gaiety
to fill up the blood, triply,
with presence.

CRÓNICA FIVE
E.S.:

*(An urgent missive written from Tokyo to Chus Pato in Lalín, Galicia,
but in the language of no one, so that it can't be read)*

I was facing the soil.
I was bent before the soil's chalk.
My soil's shadow
sudden snow and a smell of childhood:
grass fording the slough in rain, bent over
blind to collect her shadow,
her bird death no smaller with its
wings and boats in the high birches
enflamed.
For you, always, i don my disguise, ashen;
disguise of ashes that floats me
to the eternal foot of the oaks, with their tremendous *galiciană*
carbuncles and water.
Where I woke up, and the duck had risen from the slough
and grasses, the drake watching it from below,
covering its egg, her egg, warm and
plină de visuri
Fanfare of the last oration
Folds of it, unfurling where flight begins.

━━

*(Did Elisa ever mail this? Was it in the papers she left in Bucharest the
day she decamped in such a hurry? It is a scrawl on the back of a photo
of a small marsh surrounded by a northwest Calgary suburb. Stănescu
is the soil, clearly, and Pato means duck. The language of no one haunts
us. No one speaks it. No one reads it here. Or is it E.M.'s handscrawl?
In the future, her cribbing will have failed; E.M. was the one who had a*

childhood. Above the marsh or slough, an aurora. E.S.? Long absconded from her studies of 歌舞伎.

And comes the snow.)

Optimal Elegy: Aurora Borealis

To suppose a tying, affix lucre from its wandering
in the melee of a road:
To see you fleeing toward the northern light
in which i was born,
seeding fallow deer, with hooves,
in time their light widens and howls
with long sonnets alternating the night stars.

Did you see the cold at the gate!
The will to guard fell loose from my arms
as you plunged into its grip, relentlessly breathing,
lauding past all limit
the sea's animals.

Sky's ocean crests, draws out, crests again
each thread a molecule of its own cloth
catches the eye of deer and goes still,
salty
with so much more sea,
with a troop of whales it stills.

You plunge into the high waters of this sea,
without hesitation, born of Brownian privilege
inside a mask of spurs, dispersing
zigzags you love to face
and the sea, in tune with its rightful molecules,
as adept as Hercules.

You'll perhaps greet its far neck, you'll
perhaps have mercy smile on you —
no more zigzags tripled
intruding on the wound

that is a spur's destiny.

I saw you, then, flee into the northern light
in which you too were born,
howling, widening outward, robed in scintillating
venetian sky,
at the crepuscule's gates of ice
seeking respite from scintillation.

II

We learned to dabble in this light,
genuflecting at length, vertically
under the pale roseate
verge of no nation.
Yet hearing your glad tongue unties a book
i write — but in cuneiform.*
Thus it is as engineers of flowers
we scrutinize hunger's platform and are full.

Engineers, we shadow the bed,
between pages of superlatives and full of jokes,
tied under, our far wings open without rancour,
with such shudders. . . .

It was not my turn to deprive us
of that farness we make new, its crescendo,
when, virile together, rasped sadness
rubs the farthest gates until we let it go.

The aurora borealis, out there — speaks to me,
and i laud its glow of light in the highest task
arms draped, birthing cells,

never foundering as it widens the gates of wings.

Borealis, mortal zone
where marble dances,
with nothing to copy it into the stone
in which infinite grief is sculpted.

Borealis, white, — dark,
air-silver,
revelation, velvet nervature, sadness' tryst
widening and orbiting.

III

It would be ridiculous to end this poem,
surpassing the open globe of dawn
when no laughter destroys itself in our versions.

If only the sphere were in tune with mountains
and the faces of birds as they stand in their amphibian nests
with pockets of ripe grain, watching
the borealis glow!

Then the smile's ideal would not be depleted here.
For each sea, birthing amphibians, sinks
mischievous in innocence, visible to
immense vultures, their cloaks groping stone,
batting wings to rise upward, seeing up there

the passage of more seas, this above all else,
how with cartilage and bones of blue
an engineer careens and inverts
light in that timeless country, boreal, our sphere.

Then our smile's ideal would not be depleted, oh not here,
in the dawn of versions' generosity:
a much more oceanic, winged ideal.

înțeleg puțin românește

The Only Elegy I Know

If i had entered as refused wool, shoeless
where antiseptic had once touched my insides, and there
i slipped my tongue free, to unslip against
a signal tongue, singularly hers.
One sentiment united itself in my spine, coiling,
a sensation of eyes catching me in their orbit.
Oh, you, tumult of all i see,
you, oh, tasting of incremental nasturtiums.
So that i am seized by the idea,
touching the cloth that matters.
I know in myself a feeling of bliss
in every particle and date.
If even refuge contains an obelisk
that shears a heart's curvature,
you clothe my skin from harshness,
drape lips on mine and breathe,
bring me twisting
entirely encircling you with my humility.
How all this knowing
flares hotly, rotund, and solid.
To refuse my own shell, oh!
Its fluency much larger is unburrowed in the
lip of such encounter,
a bolt of day insisting adoration.
With eyes cast to see the unrealized
drape me, strike me, high and low,
born surely of the ancient reign of animals,
whom i know love so beautifully and who
almost bear my name.
My shell refused that is
yet mine, harsh wool,
now fills a much bigger oh,

cloth of a much bigger idea,
galvanized doubly, doubling passages,
passing furiously beyond jocularity.
To concentrate on ohs, how spartan they refuse
what is faithful to ruin and to parsimony.
Breathing in passages from every spore,
stratospheric and doubled ohs,
they amaze earth's many-coloured cloth,
its rhythm dilates and echoes.
Oh sight! My rasped syllable
in a perpetual crest smoothes out
the far roof of stalactites'
seduction.
Your signals circle my own signs, affirm
the eye in the ocular, and again, repeatedly
the swoosh in the swoosh, demand
the sun's entirety, such is our desire.
In an oh, in one much bigger
and at last visible, to face a nest-burrow
ripe. No more in sleep
is fidelity to each entwined, but
in the waking cloth that is never one, never one
ever again.

E.S.:

I can't believe I lost the translation I was working on in the field. I'd been trying to open up numbers as words, struggling with Stănescu's Romanian. I've looked all over for what I translated, backtracked to where the railroad tracks were torn up, behind the chipped stone wall, in case it had fallen out of my bag. It was already dusk when I got back there, and the leaves of the grasses were trembling with a pale blue light: the city's own light reflected down off the clouds into every crevice. Even the wall is luminous in its verticality. The only shadows at this late hour are those of the night people who live here. But they flatten into the wall when they see me moving, for they know I'm not one of them. They see my ache and they leave me to it.

—

I wish I could reconstitute the translation, because one poem teaches me the path of the next, and I want to go on. But when I try to go backward in time to find it, my hand just marks lines and letters in a strange outcry. Can the hand ache as the mouth does, for words?

—

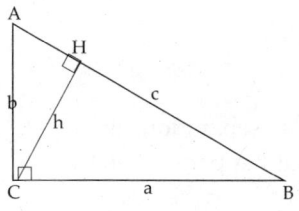

—

On the way back to my hotel, I stop briefly on Matei Voievod across from the church and look up. There's light in E.M.'s windows. They're shut tight and the curtains are drawn, but there's light there.

—

Days later I find my draft, crumpled up, in the garbage. I recognized the sheet of yellow paper, and pulled it out. My relief doesn't last long, though. It's not the poem I remember at all but one I have never seen. Whereas my draft translation had all the signs of the tripling that mark Stănescu's verse, the knots, the air of time, this poem hurls a stone from the pyramids into a void. It's like a message from O., trying to stall me in my work on the elegies. Or just telling me not to worry, that time is big. But it can't possibly be from O. After all, she's already left. Or she never came here. In any case, it's not my handwriting.

—

Yet I can't suppress a suspicion that these looped scribbles *are* the same poem. Where I struggled with: "One plus one don't make two," this version says blatantly: "The dreamy one is the original departer." It dawns on me that it's the same line, and solves the equation. For when one departs, how could there be two? The line that can't be crossed in translation is long crossed now. I can't go back. I'll just have to use this translation and go on from here.

—

"If the relation to the other presupposes an infinite separation, an infinite interruption where the face appears, what happens when another interruption comes . . . a rending interruption at the heart of interruption itself?" (J.D., on Emmanuel Levinas, *penned on a yellow page in a cramped and angular hand*)

74

The Dreamy One

The dreamy one is the original departer.
Comes from afar:
in a far frenzy,
in far protectorates of light,
and carries
from afar, insouciance.

Has insisted on coming.
Artful, fills us
with every imaginable form,
turning the three seeds of the margin
existential,
or, purely and simply,
sweetens existence
and like an aster, sunders all
that devours her.

Who knows who eats who.
The dreamy one hurls a huge pyramid
of the void
into the sea of the deserts.

Grips onto the self.
Into that sphere
and into the veritable air
and assimilates it.
Eats the frenzy,
but eats it from inside.
In the far poignancy
her inner face has teeth.
Who knows who is eaten by whom.

The dreamy one marks inconjurable fires
and what she knows of existence, she claims only

that it exists.

Mortal breath
is the earth's atmosphere.
We breathe breath's lore;
and torch breath with a finger
joined to our breathing . . .

The dreamy one stands taller
knowing mortality.

She leaves, breathing.
And the surroundings
breathe her,
objects of breath and unbreath
make air of the air.

Who knows who breathes who.
The story coalesces in these solemn words,
and victorious, never tires itself in one form of
speech,
pronouncing from the face
more perfectly than we do.

Earth "sticks" to her
and pulls breath to the earth
that "won't stick."
Who knows who is breathed by who.

The dreamy one comes and goes.
Who knows what's in her eyes
and what riches of eyes
exist in the space she returns to.

The dreamy one's retina is alive
with the riches of the retina!
Wants to be unpredictable, always,
    united by another eyelash,
    united by another eye opening,
    anothered by another eyebrow,
    another's open gaze holding her eye.
Who knows who is passing through who.

It's not her who penetrates the seed,
it penetrates directly.
Everything is alive and full.

The dreamy one comes from afar
from way-out-there or further
and is full of more departures, further than way out there.
This time she comes.
Who knows any more who is coming
and who becomes who from way out there
and, full of more departures from way out there,
    is.

All is alive and full in her:
poignancy in the poignant,
breath in breath,
aster in aster,
retina in retina.

Undrastically

I came out of the pleistocene into your beauty;
i clambered over the black wall separating
hands and light
to the shock of you,
to the shock of greeting you
with my eternal foot hanging still on the other side.
I could not speak in light,
but scrambled in its annular crags.
It pulled teeth out of its mouth
so i would not come further,
but the soft light of rapture
was mine, and mine the indefatigable foot rising.
I came out of the pleistocene into your beauty
and i could not carry myself over the wall
in such shuddered light
till i lifted my eternal foot skyward, holding
your high foot with my foot as my voice rose to your low voice
and the wall bowed
and the cattle
heard lowing, rapture lighting the sky.

Agitated Elegy

soon, M.I.M., soon

I'm blown over. In the doorway of rain,
the shoed snowflakes all fall then flee.
The organ of the invisible
finds her in her far name,
nasal, snowy
unseeing, untasting, unpalpitating
chilled in eyes and eardrum
chilled in fingers and limbs
as evening wanes in her.
It comes inveterately, more intense after a pause,
there is no sight for what comes,
it comes seeing, simply, between the lines,
there is no smell for what comes,
after taste's humid vibration
gentles harsh lips,
after the eardrum relentlessly elaborates
its mystery of the eclipse,
after palpitation and caresses, the moonlight's
intense undulation,
yearning to negate mystery,
on the far side of the face, where her name is.
But i can't call her, i'm blown over. Blown over
with something between hearing and seeing
with a feeling of eyes, a feeling of ears
never before invented.
Traipsed outside the rambling frenzy,
traipsed cherubic
raring to set space free,
doubly legible in the bones,
where its apparatus is not lessened
in the smooth organ of spheres,

between vision and hearing, between taste and sight
intent in the bliss of touches.
I'm blown over, at the chalked wall
of eye-eardrum, of tongue-sightedness.
With calculation erring
my abstract animal, yet
fleeing spirited from abstract vanities,
spirited from abstract foam.
And with the trickled print of the organ's investiture
in flesh and nerves, in eardrum and retina
leading her away to the cosmic void,
leading to the divine.
Organ in hemispheres, intense organ,
organ scraping up ideas, that races to emulate
its sphere, in the domed bone
calcinating in its calcination, her Achilles heel
where she loved and found mortal wisdom; organ
fluttering far-off
in its bone-marble, strictly,
obliterating the pain in death, by dying.

She's going, unblown in the rain
unbroken between the Polestar
and the Dogstar and the Archer
and Cassiopeia in the sky of evening.
More rain could not erase my own incapacity
that wants what rains into our apartness
expending words, in the value of root-words,
which have value.
She's going, stalled intensely in the stone and genuine tempest,
her organ heading far off, maestral,
ah, and whatever catches her, we suffer as one
in the universal intrigue.
I hurt as badly as the sea,

i'm blown over with symbols and stone,
in her four roots: of rain
of meteorites, of dill branches, of beets.
The organ named grass makes me likely to fall,
the organ named bull takes her yoke from my shoulders,
and from the fulminating bullfighter
who she is, pacing toward me, with her shoulder of sand.
The organ normally soaked dry
in torrential rain, repeats,
and the organ of the tale, repeats and intrigues,
linking us forever.
It hurts me diabolically and verbally
it hurts me in cups, in ligatures
it hurts me falling, and flowing, cherubic,
the tree of life, sawn into a decoration.
The centre of the atom hurts me
and the charred coast that holds me
hurts so i can't depart in the limit of what traipses
in the sky's traipsing, divine.
I'm blown over. The rain hurts me
where it hits my face in the doorway of the yoke and grass
where i face away from the phantasmic gesture
of the rain's own dance, slanting.
A key that can't be seen can't be suffered
key that can't be heard can't be tasted
key that can't be seen, key that does not capture
my incremental agitation,
scholastic as my island,
making light visible and simple,
enervating the high death from which all death
is invented in her, and i cannot stamp it out.

I'm not blown over from singing
or from views out of your spartan windows

i'm blown over by the numeral 1
that can't be parted again
into two breasts, two ankles
into two ears, two shoes
into two feet in big boots
that can't keep themselves from walking.
The numeral 1 that can't be shared into two eyes
two taciturnities, two struggles
two reigning laws, two hemispheres, two
martyrs lain down in two shrouds of loam,
speechless loam of rain and earth, undivine,
enumerating the numeral of the mind, 1 mind, 1 trust,
1 furrow.

The Unseizable Elegy

it will come in spring

In intimacy much bigger than our destiny in time,
we part yet in kisses
perhaps bound in parting's parting, the de-parture of parting
beyond the one,
in the disturbing rain of lava,

you, continuing in the great sea of forms, yet
knowing your own self, yet
made of enduring material whose mystery seizes me,
it seizes me that this could die.
To see this cast, as clear as any being which knows itself
whose mystery, so dear to us, comes clear
to seize morning.

To be alert in this seizure, with our inner coursing,
a gift of the stars that traverse more intensely in us
to enter our breath
strenuously as the me begins its story, as you
turn back through the turnstile to your glad oasis,
seeding matter
strenuously
as my words wrap the ache of absence
so my head will no longer see.

Or to be alert as we can, for what we yet feel inside us.
I'll be alert, for what can no longer be
named in the uprising
from the mists of possibility,
yet is no more than what is singular in itself
and, unsuspecting, knows itself, narrated intimately;
its future predicates so powerfully arrayed in the coursing that

centres us,
spartan as a planet released to spin its size against the pitons
of feeling and of plants,
is,
intense as knowing, as the pyramid
that unites us triply in every single strand.

II

All is simple. Touches simplicity. Fully
divines the unfathomable.

All is touched closely, is touched
by closeness, filled
with the tragedy of the seer
who is never again seen.

All is touched perfectly
in spring,
though unconjurable in this cold, i
constantly know
it will arise from grass that will rise anew to witness
words from mouths that utter them,
witnesses of the mouths' intimacy
which is intimacy's inner well,
that in itself seizes shyly what
is of the earth,
and which implicates us without judging:
the infinity of my arms risen against gravity

to hold yours without relenting
in the embrace's powerful touch,
fully serene in arms' mystery.

III

Here every parting alerts us in the plurality of *you*,
seeded as one, in the hourglass:
where, in every parting, at once
there is the clamour of the fall and,
above it, a twice-fallen silence.

IV

The cloth of the unknown alerts us with this *you*, waning,
what we cannot see yet of its weave
and what spins light outward, independent of our features
helps us to think out fruitfully the seeds we will let grow,
for the weave that alerts us knows
the cherishing seized in all alerts, in all knowledge.
I see myself fallen into this *you*
as it arises in us, in the tenderness of seeds
irrepressible as they are beloved.

V

If i was not duped in letting such happiness
enter me,
was i then duped
mistiming the vast signs
that had melted stone? Or
that held in my embrace were just mercurial
twinned over and over,
risen in mirrors?
Time, so big, worked to deprive my voice
of the embrace it had assumed,

all lustre, all glow in those days of odes
i did speak toward her.
They were to me hazard's just accomplishment, yet not duped in
all they set aglow in me,
now past, and yet so much is still glowing.

VI

So i remain
steadfast in what i am,
my mouth steady in solitude, shielded from cold,
assuming my own happiness
i shake off the preterit
to don what is ahead
in myself, again, what is to the right, and yet
to the left of me, above and yet
under me, placating
the preterit so ruined
preterit that still makes me sweet and light:
sky —— stars,
earth —— air,
shadow —— hers, burst into leaf.

VII

. . . it gnaws me too much, is too asymmetrical,
hard to be insouciant
in the sphere of her presence.

To see her is to stand in the fate of the sun,
its eventual explosion as a star,

and to step with daring into the increase in light,
more light than can ever reassure me.

VIII

To spring from our own earth
in the very sowing of such light; though winter
now ices lichen at the oasis of our dawn, spring
will write the length of laughter.

Springing from my own centre
when, human and alone, i'm haunted
by the net of love,
or purely and simply when winter
falls away and spring
is misting space in a wide circle
seeding hearts intimately
with the space of love's own unseizable margins.
Amazingly there is a cure
in spring,
the knowledge of seeds that speak life in the sowing
as earth speaks already of earth.

But more urgent than anything
we *are* seeds, we are
what wanders in all partings still,
and our place is also in the light that streams from eyes
or from a field, the field of grasses
grown before our eyes — us with our ourness
not yet undone, though some say it hardens as do molten metals,
yet we still sow fire with our beings
to help us work in work's torrent
in the place of cherished tremors

in which
our work yet is to be born.

More urgent than anything
we are seeds, and implicated
in the rising of our own selves as we hazard a way outward
to where exaltation rises,
to where parting bears the name of spring.
To be in being and laud the phenomenal, again and again
laud the phenomenal.

To be yet in being
these seeds spring up for us, unseizable
in our own earth.

PART TWO

The Paul Celan Translations by Erin Moure

———

*tampered into English
from the English of Oana Avasilichioaei's
translations of Paul Celan's Romanian poems,
which she showed me*

*para M.I.M., coas últimas palabras que aprendeu ela:
"ce frumoasă este viața"*

CRÓNICA SEVEN
E.M.:

The book's been open on my desk for days, other books on top of it, a coffee drip, crumbs of a cracker. When I lift my eyes back to it and see the words, they deafen me. I have to get up and shut the window. The racket off Matei Voievod is tremendous at times, reverberating between high stone walls from the narrow passage of the street. Cars, beer trucks, the recycling truck, refrigerated trucks of milk, all pass below my window. And schoolchildren. And those heading onto Strada Austrului to shop or eat. The only way I can sleep is to close the window. I bring the book with me.

Outside the glass, the roar of the street, the murmur of the inhabitants in evening, the dirt rising from the pavements, is still that of Matei Voievod, even when I am not there to witness it.

—

The Celan translations have become impossible. My translated line "Spoke a leaf" is Galego, not Celan. The subject tailing its verb. The ache in my mouth and throat is such that even English emerges giddy, in Galego. As if English, the old tongue of no one, tongue of us all, gibberish I had lived in since childhood, scrubs off. Spoke a leaf. In fact, no leaf speaks since they cut down the tree outside my window last week. Now the racket is even louder, on Saturday night, especially, without the wall of foliage.

—

I threw it in the paper recycling right after extracting it from the mailbox in the lobby. The kind of postcard printed *en masse* by realtors to crow their triumphs. A sunlit building with an X marked on a high corner apartment, and an intense blue sky.

When I walked out later, the card was still lying on top of the box. So I pulled it out. Perhaps it was for an art opening, I admonished myself, flipping it over. The ink-scrawled address on the verso left no space for a message. Yet the address is message enough. Instead of E.M., it is addressed to E.S. My heart sinks. Her last name misspelled or smudged, as Sampedrinu. But the civic numbers are unmistakable: my own address on rue Rachel in Montreal. Postmarked just over a year ago. I have no clue how this card made its way today to the row of brass mailboxes in the lobby on Matei Voievod. The sky in it is blue, entirely blue. I'm stumped. But something about the X marked on the photo intrigues me. A slight jag in one of the diagonals.

O.

I brought the card upstairs. But I already knew that if I checked the postcard of the department store, Muntenia, and its street of apartments, I'd confirm that the X on each card was marked on the same building. With the same jag in the cross. I was sure of it. So I didn't look.

—

I'd heard nothing from O. during that first absence in Romania, though I knew she'd gone to Bucharest to finish her Stănescu translations, the ones she later published as *Occupational Sickness*. She returned almost exactly a year later. She wasn't in touch then either. I found out about her return from the painter, her friend. He was a bit startled that I hadn't seen her, but didn't try to insist. He saw the look on my face.

Was she really back? I looked at the phone, but it was late so I quelled the impulse.

—

"When friendship begins before friendship, it touches upon death, indeed, it is born in mourning . . . And already from its birth: in all the books of questions, those that bear and those that keep their name silent, beyond books and their titles, beyond blind words. Books are here to no avail, no more than questions are, not to mention answers." (Jacques D., *after the death of Jabès*)

—

Suddenly I have no saliva. I sit up in the bed. All I want is to swallow and I can't swallow. The gulp pains me. My insides are still shocked. The paragraph, the whole paragraph in front of me, has been circled carefully in pencil.

But I haven't read this far yet. This is the first time I've opened the book to this page. And I bought it new, unbroken, unread.

Not only is the paragraph circled, but she's scribbled the word "foşnet" in the margin.

I have to fall asleep before the stale heat gets to me. For although the window onto the stradă is shut tight to allow sleep, it can also forbid it.

—

I woke up thinking of the spam photo of the woman with the low wagon or handcart and ludicrous packages in the concrete suburb. With E.S. and O., caught at random on the far edge, carrying a sofa in the distance. I took out yesterday's card depicting the apartment building and flipped it over. O.'s handwriting, E.S.'s name.

—

They had met in that very apartment. Cooking dinner. Eating canapés and lounging on that sofa.

—

That's a stupid thought, I realize. It's not dinner time. But O. had sent this postcard, with the jagged mark across a high balcony, to Elisa, to advise her of something. Without words. It had to be something they'd already talked about.

I realize the absurdity of what I've just said. They didn't know each other, and could not have met. O. had simply sent it to me, and made some kind of mistake in the name. But it perturbs me so much I can't swallow my coffee.

—

Dear E.: Dinner at 8, if you are free, next Thursday. I am sure I can help you with your research then. I've moved since I came back, I hope you don't find it too far and too suburban. O.
Dear O.: Should I bring your notebook? E.
Dear E.: Notebook? But it's me who has your notebook, or a page from it. I'm saving it for you, don't worry. O.
Dear O.: . . . E.

—

Two can play at this game of no messages.

—

94

"The night's blanket sewn up around the shoulders." I want to ask O. about that line in her Celan. I'm having so much trouble getting it right, in English from her English, without losing its sonority. The line makes me ache so. "Night's blanket sewn up around her shoulder." I'm not sure yet. But I've written the Thursday date in my agenda under *Xoves*. I can wait until then.

—

The human eye is more acute than the camera lens. For one thing, it chooses what to ignore in a scene, without our even knowing it. How I could look across the long river valley in the city where I was born and not even see the suburb in the foreground. Yet when I print the photograph, a jumble of boxy houses fills the frame and the valley behind is too small to distinguish.

I would have walked right by that apartment in Bucharest. Maybe I already had.

—

It's been a hot day. Couldn't work inside. Out here in this field, the ragged tree no longer has a sofa at its roots. And some of the night people must have burned the wooden benches for warmth and light, for blackened sticks of milled wood lie in a fire pit. Green grass is sprouting amid the matted brown from last year. I'm on my chunk of cement where I usually sit. This is the only place I can be calm. I've brought my Celan papers. "Tomorrow's laugh is autumn's walnut, touch today the dew," O. had written. I don't know what to make of it. The windowed bulk of the textile factory looms mere metres away, a comforting presence that blocks the horizon. Up on the seventh floor, someone is looking out, but not at me.

I just feel that old hurt in my mouth again, as if my face is becoming unrecognizable, even to me. The feeling in it.

The machine-noise snags in the blue fabric of the air.

—

"There is something in translation that precedes that first mark, the letter. A kind of space. But not a space that's blank, rather, a kind of febrility. The space exactly prior to the letter, before the letter enters the field." I have to shake O.'s handwriting out of my head and stop reading her notebook. I wish she would come to get it, but I haven't heard any more from her. I'll bring it back to her on Thursday.

—

Holes in the fence lead from the field to where the night people now live, in a kind of shed just high enough for raising rabbits or pigs, behind a low concrete building with no windows. New grass has grown right through the shattered wood of their house of last summer, by the tree. This is where I like to sit in the afternoon. You never see the night people at that hour, just their traces. Mostly I watch the birds in the scrub willow, and the two poplars that have grown unimpeded for years.

—

The factory workers start to stream out at 4 p.m.; some of the paths are theirs. They carry nylon or poly lunch bags and sweaters; they're almost all immigrants, from nowhere around here. Their paths lead to the subway station where they disperse. The only people who are from here are the night people. They lead different lives, holed up in the weeds, with cold and garbage.

I'm at ease out in the field and on its paths — the women who fabricate textiles walk through here; it's what they first see upon leaving their jobs for the day. They traverse it while monastery bells ring down the road behind a wall, across from the freight doors of the place where chicken pieces were made out of chickens, back when the railway was here.

—

"It would be necessary to accede or do justice to this torsion of the time of reading. At once painful and fascinated, it calls or recalls in advance a sort of living present, or what is assumed to be so, that is, our own living present, toward the other fractured present of the one who, having written this book . . ." (Jacques D.)

Reading Derrida in the field at 4 p.m., I begin to realize what draws O. back to her own field, to the work she does, and did. She isn't one of the night people.

—

(found in O.'s notebook by E.M.)

"It turns out there are other triplings: tongue, cortex, light. In translation, this plurality acutely matters. The stimulation of the tongue by the word is electro-tactile, and I am sure it activates the visual cortex, not just the language centres. Thus altering space itself, for space is a relation with the body.

"Just as braille reading activates the striate and extrastriate cortices in blind people, putting the word to be translated into the mouth causes significant changes in several areas of the brain that process space and light, *ergo* vision. Could it also be that this plurality can reverse time? Or detain it?

"I need to speak to E. She seems agitated these days. She sits up there in that apartment with the windows shut, claiming she is working. It would do her good to get out and see the sky."

Map of Calgary

UN

I touched the fur on her head, her head bowed, she at the edge of the bed, sitting bowed, I touched her hair, full resonance, the bell.

Flag lashing against the pole, no rain.

I leaned and touched her head, she did not look at me.

She touched my palm with her hair.

The flagropes tremored.

Spoke a leaf.

The herald of sheep's coats.

(When I look up: a small thread, an alarm bell.)

DOUS

The smallest of white curls, I look close, smile.
Ramses is in the flowerpots (an email from the pyramids).

She touches her rib cage, gingerly,
to her right: it's hurting here now.

I am given over to language.

The seeds of the cosmos grow up as poppies, I suggest.

Red poppies, she asks?

The flagropes still, sunlit. No noise on the metal.
I'll open that door when I come to it, I tell her.

She lies back. This feels right, feels better.

A ribprint on my hand. I save it.

(A coyote in pixels. To show her.)

TRES

On the right side, the rash over the shoulder blade.
Curvature and trust.

This in the spine's bone. (Listening.)

There is no word, not even one from on high, that has any right. . . .

Her knees up, sideways, stabilize space here, such
thin arm.

When you look at the clouds she says, (Speaking.)
you can see images.

I saw the two dogs playing, the dark one held the light one down.
Then a cat came.

The curve and tilt of that vertebral column. Press it. Press it again.

That feels good, she says.

When I look at her, then, now,
what image?

CATRO

Solemnity lives here.
A quiet word glimmers

in dark space as the creams are worked in. This helps
the itch, she says.

Magpies rise out of the aspens, a truck door clangs
shut. The duck slough clots with midsummer grasses,
green swaths awaiting dusk rain.

She waits near these hills. To the right of the spine's curve
and over the shoulder, one small stitch
blue where the skin is missing.

Someday these aspens will be mowed under?

Torn sideways by the blade of machines?
And if she can't see it?

To touch aspen. Rises the leaf smell. Flag's clatter.
Just like that. In memory: *a map is what appears.*

CINCO

In the photo, her thin arms, hands held over her eyes.
She is playing the role of "see no evil."

There is one person on each side. Both look
outward. One, young, is not listening. One, older,
is not speaking.

I look at her thin arms.
Her shoulders lost in the folds of her dress.

The dress I bought with her before the blindness. Its colour.
We walk out of the store to the Walmart parking lot and breathe
fresh air.

Now she listens to the radio in the hospice and speaks of New Orleans.
In the weeks since I wrote "in the photo," I've thrown it away.

She speaks and I listen, watching.

When a blind person holds their hands over their eyes
to face us,
what are we asked to see?

SIX

Each day I touch my own face and hear the
flag.

I walk her last walk of October through the suburb past the duck
slough to the Co-op store.

Autonomy does move us here.
Solace a word. Light's funnel and
the crevices of light we enter now.

"What time is it?" she asked on the Saturday. *Cinci și cinci,*
I answered.

In me is a hard shell the size of a walnut, under the left ribs.
When it presses, I am in the water.
You who maketh the long journey.

"Does it hurt?" I asked.
She opens her mouth. This means *thank you,* or *no.*

(or I am in the river)

(wading fiercely)

(there is no shore)

SEVEN

I crossed to her between the high field and the lights of the city.
I crossed where the brown deer cross at night from the hill into the
backyards of Calgary,

Alberta, Canada, Western Hemisphere, The World.

Above me, Orion:
constellate here.

My hand held cupped to her furred cranium, still
until the warmth
goes.

And I look down
And comes the snow.

OPT

Found you in the field. At first sight
you are a white bag blown into the bushes.

And me the one blind now, unable to see clear.

So I do what we once did with the photo of the coyote
that I brought to where you were sleeping,
on the screen that helps the blind to see.

I zoom in.
It is you who are the coyote. Do you see you running?

You are in the field of late summer grasses. You look like you are
praying, but there are too few pixels to know for sure.

You are wearing (there is a shadow) the huge dark glasses.
Your arms are forward.

I know by the grass and by your arms that you are picking berries.
This knowing is a proof of memory, incised in the forever that is
who I am.

No one took this picture.
It occurs in the future, where I first touch it.

This is a map of Calgary, I unfold it to find you.
Coyote. Mère.

----

*(To be so technical that all emotion is abraded, and so clear that the poem is utterly
obscure. As a map is. And as each map contains a mistake to identify its maker, so here too.)*

CRÓNICA EIGHT
E.S.:

Again this book of grief that I open only randomly, to disturb myself, seems curiously to be describing Stănescu, or O., who for me is, in a sense, Stănescu, for she gave me Stănescu, without even knowing me. That's writing for you. Without even knowing me, this gift.

"In other words, this *there*, this *right there*, which they hold at a distance to disrupt an identification that they unconsciously fear, is also, right here, the place of their *unbeknowing*, to wit, that which they are here and now unwittingly in the process of becoming — according to the process of life and the process of translation, two processes to which they are, in all the sense of this word, *exposed, three times* exposed without knowing it: exposed to gazes or looks when they believe themselves to be looking, exposed as mortals, as living beings destined to die, and exposed in the notebook as a work of translation and by the work of translation." (J.D., *speaking of Sarah Kofman and her work on Rembrandt's Anatomy Lesson*)

I realize I've altered the quote in reading it. "Painting" to "notebook" and "art" to "translation."

It was the *three times exposed* that got to me. O.'s triplicity of language.

I no longer know if I've come to seek out Stănescu's poetry or to wait for O.

⸺

As soon as I'd flung my suitcase down in the hotel after my return from Călărași, I had to get outside and come back to the field here.

It's not summer yet but the factory windows are all flung open. The machines have gone silent, it's late in the day. It feels a bit eerie. I'm glad to get away from translation, which makes my mouth ache, and though I try to transfer it to my hands, the ache still creeps up on me. To tie up a loose end in one place unravels three others. I get too excited. I need calm.

—

On the bus back, I'd read the strangest article. Or maybe it's obvious. Turns out the tongue can be activated to see. Given a camera port linked up to microelectrodes on its wet surface, the tongue carries a charge easily, receives visual information through a strip of red plastic from the camera-machine, and transmits this info through nerve fibres to the brain. The part of the brain that processes visual information is activated by this transmission: the brain doesn't care if its visual impressions don't come from the eye. So the tongue can see. Speak too. But, also, see.

—

If I could take the camera I found at Autogara Obor on Bd. Gării de Est in București and hook it up to my tongue, I'd see what E.M. sees. Or saw when she took the photos. As if it were me seeing for the first time. I'd have that exact sensation. That's how translation wants to feel. Wants to, and can't. Its transmission always sputters. Its ache takes over the whole body. Me in București to translate Stănescu from Romanian into English. Because of O. Though I know no Romanian.

Yet, that's how I feel when I read Stănescu. O. read it before I did, in Romanian. Now I read what she read, the Romanian, and to the right, her English. In fact, there is no camera between me and O. There are words. It's more direct, it hits you harder.

Stănescu says the tongue is just the far end of the intestine, turned inside out. A sort of reverse anus. That's what reading wants to do, turn you inside out. The *there* and the *here*. The tongue and the visual cortex and the anus. And you, reader, in the middle. Tripled. Smelling of chalk and skin.

—

For the record, I'm jubilant. At last! When I went back to O.'s translation after doing one of mine this afternoon, sitting in the ragged field by the textile plant, I found blood in hers where there was blood in mine. At last. After so long struggling with my incomprehension of Romanian, I was able to translate star as star instead of as stone. At last I did not feel so bereft. I looked down at the raggedy grasses at my feet. Laid-down, dusty, paper caught in them. As if an entire winter's snow has just melted, and the light touches their crushed stems for the first time this year.

I'm shaking a bit. It can't be helped. O. is long gone from Bucureşti, but I am starting to find her. Blood, grass, stone. Triplicity. It strikes me now that O. will be back. I feel it in the chest. Two lungs, a heart, the trio of breath, and O. will be back.

Life, *simplu. Viață*, simply. *Ce frumoasă este viața.*

—

Yet when I translate Stănescu, it's my death I think of. When he starts out that breath poem with: "One day it came to me suddenly," I don't have to read further to know what he's talking about. O. translated that same line with the word "angel" in it. This word surprised me. But, on reflection, I decided her translation was faithful: we were referring to the same thing.

—

"Dear E.: My Stănescu is finished, finally, and I'll be back in a few days. I've been out of the capital to read the manuscript in my field and make the final changes in the translation. I see in the field what I don't see elsewhere. When you get this, call me, and I'll know you're back in town too. O."

That's what I'd thought was in the looped scrawl on the back of O.'s postcard. I hadn't bothered to read it: I stole it for the photo of the field. The message wasn't intended for me anyhow. It was intended for E.M. But now I craned to decipher the handwriting, and pulled back, astonished at what I was reading, the letters visualized in my mouth before they registered via my eyes.

—

"Dear E.: At times the purple light is lain so low unto the field that I leave the grasses to speak the wind's word, and these grasses then enter my writing from up above, in the window. From here where I sit, I see how the footpath shines out, calling light into it when the moon rises, a path of silver that could be water that starts far off in the field to wend its way up and into my own shoulder and down into my arm, surely.

"I know too I am not the only one who watches this field. In the purple before dawn or in the drawing down of night, there is too the wink of houses, a grey wall of an apartment block, wires, a street, garages, a muddy crease of yard with its utterances of metal and the gazes of those who sort there the bits of rust and jointings to sell or melt again. And, too, the dogs who pull the blanket of the night close and keep it here for hours with their throats ever open in that unending cry dogs make. The roosters take the sky back from them in the morning. For there is a sky invisible to the camera, that I see but the camera cannot, a raucous sky that hums with factory, a sky that has brushed its hem along the earth until sky too is tinged with foot-trodden earth that is mud and metal, and this is sky, too, dear E. I return tomorrow; when you get this, call me and I will know you're in town too. O."

I turned the card back over and realized I hadn't looked properly at the photo before, either. It showed no field at all but a lit window and the dusk lain low across a landscape that would not reveal itself to me but for the glint in the darkness of a house or two, a wire. Looking at the card now, I understood what E. was saying about the camera. And I suddenly realized that here was a way I could find O.

—

My chest hurts when I read what I have done. The right bronchial, my heart too, all my insides ache and the wave crests in the mouth which hurts too. I see what I have done and I am terrified by it. I want to write to O. I need to tell her I am terrified. I don't know her but I have to at this moment. How did it occur that I translated what O. translated as "earth-shattering death" by "the short moratorium we have from death"? It terrifies me that the Stănescu could murmur to me and insist on such vocabulary from me when it is the opposite of what he had written for O.

I put my head out the window. I hope there is enough air out there to breathe again. I feel that I have sunk into a well and that it will break me into tears if I don't speak to her.

Dear O.

I can't write her yet, I can't write her yet.

. . .

. . .

. . .

⎯⎯

It turns out on my return that E.M.'s field is easy to find in Montreal. It has in it both immigrants and, high up in a pale blue sky, two birds. On the zoom, I can look at it closely, pixel by pixel. I'd taken the photo myself with E.M.'s camera. The field could be the field in Călărași, but there's an alien flag in one corner, blue and white. A chicken processing plant is closed in the background, weedy grass pushing up through the cracked asphalt of its truckyard. The photograph does not let you hear the bells from the monastery across the way. E.M. always talks about the poplars being the highest thing in that field, but you can't always believe E.M. And in this case, the camera shows she's wrong: the building, a textile factory, looms much higher. I print the photo and take up a pencil. It's a 14-floor building, and on the 7th floor a window is open. I mark an X there. Now you can't see the figure looking out and down, you just see the mark.

I send the photograph to O., at her last known address.

Poetry's Arithmetic

reading solemn markings

One plus one don't make two,
one plus one makes three,
are four, are five.
An intrepid one plus a soft one
makes a camellia.
That seven embraces will make one
makes a dozen plus one,
makes five and four
is nine, and one is 10, makes chalk.
I opt to make three,
to touch the wall, first, so
my new hand can double me
with life.

A poet knots the word.

A poet knots the victorious.

I sleep and dream in Iranian subtitles
and air is time's intermediary
entering the present victoriously intact.
Air *is* time's intermediary
entering the present imperfect
though it was May before the verb made time stop for Nietzsche.
There exists a grammar of numbers,
1 poet is the subject
gifting 1 poet with the predicate.
1 poet makes a cloth of the sun
and gives 1 poet this cloth
of light.
1, 2, 3,
the goat, an ox, a twirl
goats (how many?)

twirls (how many?)
ox (the one, the one)

Scoop by 1

Glide by 1
gift piquancy in 1.

— To add any more, you'd need Pythagoras' spoon!

— I'm not adding! The earth's so flat when a girl lies flat,
and what an omelette.

This 1 girl can vex an animal
from the singularity of its glass casing.
Right into the talent of tomorrow
with doubled piquancy. This numeracy
and a dream, a voice uttering this dream as a slogan,
2 tarrying naked totals 2 softly,
2 with lungs naked totals 2 in skirts
and this penetrates enrapt
and is 1, all 1
from this we know 2 equals 1
(1 is never in itself 1!),
1 in the vocative
taking its coat off at the sight of the 1,
the imperative 1!

Mathematics writes itself with a cipher, its cloth of light
gifting poetry nakedly so it can take up words.

¡Coraxe!

E.M.:

"What we know, blaze knows" are the words written on the back of the latest card. No address. But it's no ad this time, no spam. It's O.'s handwriting. And no need of an address for it wasn't delivered, I found it outside Piața Iancului on Thursday, at the subway stop nearest my apartment on Matei Voievod, right at the entrance. I had almost taken the wrong train, confused as usual by the signs, and had walked back out to reorient myself under the sky. O.'s pen. I had that feeling again of the cables letting go the elevator cabin and plummeting me seven floors to the ground.

In the subway, I could hardly keep my eyes off the photo. It is a photo of a blaze: an intense blue sky. But the blaze is not the sky, no, the sky itself is undistinguishable in the background of the photo, perhaps cloudy, with sun glinting through. The soaring blaze, is, rather, an entirely blue sky sweeping across a huge billboard, which is planted high in a sea of yellow quack grass, near a hedge swollen and unruly, at the edge of a residential street full of families walking, one yellow taxi in the road caught in passage, the face in it not visible in the glare rebounding from the windscreen. But the billboard. With leaves of a tree in full leaf shadowed across it, magnifying the blue of the sky.

My heart stops. The blaze drinks me in, making me part of the mad crescendo of street, balconies, windows, cars that frame it. The commotion of all that is outside the sky. It is surely O.'s suburb, where I am headed for dinner.

—

But the sky! I know that sky well, it is the exact sky I look into when I lean back in my chair on my roof terrace in Montreal and gaze upward. My hands hurt, holding the photo, as the subway races into the dark.

How did O. get our roof sky to a street in Bucharest?

—

I changed lines at Eroilor without even noticing, and barely had the presence of mind to get up and move through the crush of people to the doors when the voice announced, in that voice of subways all over the world: *"Armata Poporului. Atenţie, se închid uşile! Urmează Gorjului."*

—

But when I'd walked through the long aisle of marble pillars at A.P. and up onto the stradă, there was no such billboard. I was relieved. Just storefronts, a bread factory, a sign indicating a shopping centre. I take out the map on which I'd marked my own directions. And pat my pocket. They're still there; my Celan translations with the line: "What dispute did the verb make in you?"

It is a question I need to ask O.

—

Two turns later I am on a street far older. It must once have been a village road, now engulfed by the capital, for the building walls are curved as if the street follows an old brook, long dried up, diverted, or underground. I pass a green arch with books in the window and a sign, I'm a bit early anyhow, so I duck inside. Maybe I'll find some Celan in Romanian.

—

"The strange rupture has to do with translation too — this opening of the very letter. To convey a difference in tone in one language at the very instant it crosses the threshold into the other. So that the reader can't but feel it. The other language enters their own mouth as source, for an instant, blinding them to all other notice or realization."

(O.'s notebook. O. and her incredible threshold.)

"What is it, this organ, the mouth? When you turn it to take in the word, so that it touches the space in the letter? To translate is to harken to everything that comes out of this body. How do I know how the word entered? How can I truly say that any of it is really mine?"

(I no longer knew if she'd left it or if I'd pilfered it.)

—

Seeing me enter, the woman at the counter stops eating out of her bowl and gets up, vanishes. I hear clattering in the back. I look around the shop a bit, it smells like musty paper. I watch dust falling in the beam of light from the window. A dog comes out from the back to look at me, then turns and goes in again. Its claws need cutting; I can hear them hit the floor as it walks. When the woman emerges, she's already decided she doesn't wish to speak to me. Then she decides she does. Or she doesn't, for she doesn't speak, she thrusts a book over the counter into my hand. My head jerks down. Its title is in the language of my childhood in Calgary, but it's no book you'd find in Calgary readily, nor that you'd expect to find here. It's translated into the tongue of no one. *A Work on Mourning*. From French. Water running over blue stones on the cover, no sky. Utterly no sky.

Water and stone. Watergrove.

The woman counts out what she wants from my handful of coins and bills. I'm not that early any more, so I pick up my pace a bit once I'm out the door. There's still a ways to walk, if I can just follow her directions.

But I'm shaking, and I wish I could sit down.

CRÓNICA TEN
E.M.:

When I turn into the passageway of houses, narrow and long, there's a wall at the end, images painted on it. I will have to turn around, for I clearly can go no further, there's no exit. The images are human figures, as if there were no wall, a trompe d'oeil. One figure stands, arms up. Both of them are outlines, one in profile as on a Greek vase and one facing me, la gorgón, with the very stance of E.S. beckoning. The profiled figure watches her beckon. It could only be O. I must have taken a wrong turn, to end up in this long and narrow passage. I take out my camera and snap a picture. No one would believe me otherwise.

—

"Consider, then, what would be the manner of the release and healing from these bonds and this folly if in the course of nature something of this sort should happen to them. When one was freed from his fetters and compelled to stand up suddenly and turn his head around and walk and to lift up his eyes to the light, and in doing all this felt pain and, because of the dazzle and glitter of the light, was unable to discern the objects whose shadows he formerly saw, what do you suppose would be his answer if someone told him that what he had seen before was all a cheat and an illusion, but that now, being nearer to reality and turned toward more real things, he saw more truly?"

I didn't realize Plato had written about translation until I read this.

—

Camera safely stowed, nestled beside the book, a quick check of my map shows I am in fact on the right route. So I go forward. When I get nearer to the arch at the end of the passage, there are no figures. Just an opening, and dazzling light. There is the sound of barking, and a banging pot on a balcony. The dog goes quickly quiet. Light glints off the walls. Barracks and a man shouting, and then the dogs again. All writing passes through this needle. Chus Pato said that. As if Adorno is right, and *"there is no word, not even one word from on high. . . ."*

To quell the clamour, I take out my Celan notes and sit down on the steps in front of an apartment block. Then O. appears from around the corner.

My voice. Stuck in my *mou*

—

O. sits down behind me, a couple of steps higher up. She's wearing a dress the amazing colour of sky and she's looking at me, amused. Across from us on the street, a woman rattles a handcart among the parked cars. It teeters with a ludicrously huge wrapped bag and several piled boxes.

Dear O., I say, scarcely audible in the noise and not daring to look up at her.
Dear E. she says.

I'm a bit early, I say, my voice funny; I thought I'd sit a bit before finding your building.

O. laughs. I came out to find you. I thought you might get lost with the directions I gave you. Come on, she says, there's someone I'd like you to meet, and dinner's almost ready, I have to get back, I left her stirring the pot. You can sit down there on the sofa.

Oh no. I balk, then gulp, and follow O.

—

Dear O.: "And if, said I, someone should drag him thence by force up the ascent which is rough and steep, and not let him go before he had drawn him out into the light of the sun, do you not think that he would find it painful to be so haled along, and would chafe at it, and when he came out into the light, that his eyes would be filled with its beams so that he would not be able to see even one of the things that we call real?" *Love, Plato.*

—

Her hair blows lightly in the wind of Montreal.

I like that, it makes me feel happy, I lean back in my chair. We're on the roof again, and I'm hoping to show O. my translations today from Celan. She's talking avidly about Bucharest, looking up at the sky in those sunglasses, and talking about some hilarious letter she had received about E.S., who apparently had fled a dinner, leaving a pot burning on the stove and almost causing a sofa to catch fire.

Then she hands me the photo. I reach out to take it, and lean forward in my chair, squinting in the stark light of the roof to see what it depicts. There's an old passageway, narrow and peeling, buildings high on either side, tilting inward. Walls painted pink and green, with shutters and windows thrown open. Blue sky visible above.

I really can't breathe: in the far archway I recognize two shadows. E.S., surely. Her arms are flung outward and high. O. beside her.

In the window above the archway, another figure is scarcely visible, looking through glass down the passage, directly into the lens of the photographer, whom of course we cannot see.

I look up, not knowing what to say to O. The sun blinds me. Below the roof, the din on Matei Voievod is tremendous.

The fire engine is turning up the street again, blaring its horn.

. . ∴ a "force renewed" through the very renunciation of all restitution,
all reconstitution, all postmortem retribution:
the gift itself.
(J.D.)

"break simply with grief's cane"

---

the impossibility itself of the translation she was attempting.
leaping into the map of Celan's words with no instrument for
scale, for not knowing the language she instead drank words.
when she walked uphill the water followed her. because of O.A.,
Celan's words had come to her in English, the language of no one.
the language she herself could scarcely hold without it tremoring
her. so she tried to make the instrument of equivalencies, of
valence, of scale with the lines of the poems themselves:

stained petal you extinguished   =   *rose wrenching the shoulder light*

slowly unfasten grief's doves   =   *with explorers of heightitude, the hands*

but she had mixed up gloves and doves.

KEY TO READING "Two Accurate Translations of One and the Same Poem by Paul Celan"*

impetuously beautiful   =   our single shipwreck, transparent

literally: impetuous shipwreck

sky's flag   =   one floor below us silica

literally: flag below us floor

stained petal you extinguished   =   rose wrenching the shoulder light

literally: shoulder petal extinguish rose

*this poem is a monstrosity, but not a lie.

"The human soul applies this excess of forces to the formation of language."
Heymann Steinthal, 1851

"The deportations began the following day." Paul Celan

Two Accurate Translations of One and the Same Poem by Paul Celan

Great Southern Cross

impetuously beautiful
sky's flag
stained petal you extinguished
ash those nights
stain its silver in blood
blaze announce
there, unspeakably

(when boat reaches shore, the oars stop

(no way to become trees again

(rose wrenching the shoulder dark

(panther gashed dawn

Tropic

our single shipwreck, transparent
one floor below us silica
rose wrenching the shoulder light
ash those nights
kissed her incestuous
blaze announce
flood of light creasing the window

(I climbed one of the arms of light

(laid down oars to fathom

(boat-marks tugged into snow

(gaze vacant with walnuts save themselves

Wing

ash those nights
blaze renounce

"contagious fire and hours that break all clocks"

"slowly unfasten grief's doves"

their wing-harrows
their salt tears

"she stepped over the threshold to face an eyelid"
so that i could get up and breathe at ease,
arrest the hour from time's conflagration

a poem now to be assembled in any order, by anyone's hand

4, "mourning drunk from a palm"
   staggers not a bit of it
   the palm opens clamour so leafed, rested

2, barefoot to be told
   steps rambles
   walk through the long brown grasses

1, "ash that night"
   (snow alight)

3, "but how it floats amidst grasses with outstretched wings!"
   Shoulder, face, wing:
   I *éclate* you out of the waters.

encántame o recendo da menta nos teus dedos . . .

(we travellers of images blind

(next to you: transform colour

my	*wing-harrow*
salt-	*wether*
loam,	*azul*
*	
(with explorers of heightitude	the hands

Living Proof (original)

this lexicon is Paul Celan's and Oana Avasilichioaei's, i arrested it.

Boat, face, wing:
night's blanket sewn up around her shoulders.

Our convulsive foam
glove's nocturnal kiss:
oar in the high birches enflamed

The palm's open clamour is
leafed sky, rested
barefoot to be told

steps brambles   *but what we know, blaze knows*
"walk through the long brown grasses"
"ash that night"
(endure)

Tomorrow's laugh is autumn's walnut, touch today the dew
"how it floats amidst grasses with outstretched wings"

⇀ break harrow ⇀ simply ⇀ grief's cane ⇀

CRÓNICA ELEVEN
E.M.:

E.S. on a rooftop. E.S. with one shoulder bare and grinning, on a rooftop. A table on a rooftop with E.S. grinning. Sunglasses, and red tiles behind her. E.S. in front of a monstrous dish of *xeado*, on a roof terrace, red-tiled, terraced fields, a city centre soaring on the horizon. E.S. smiles at the photographer. About to eat a giant ice cream.

I click the red button and set the camera down. The tiny LED screen goes dark.

—

When O. gave me back my camera on the roof of the building at the corner of Rachel and Henri-Julien, saying matter of factly it had been found at the bus station, I'd taken it from her hand, surprised and delighted to see it again.

O. reclined in a chair looking up at the sky, hair blowing gently around her face, watching two gulls soar in the air above. Not looking at me at all.

Azul is blue in Galego, I tell her, a bit aimless, putting the camera down, gazing too into the sky. At that moment I felt such ache and tenderness, that threshold rose in me all over again, I looked upward, too, my mouth ached with a sweetness I could not identify, and the word came to me then in another language, in my own language, E.S.'s language, I didn't want to say it, a wonderful word: *Quérote.* _____, O., I said, looking up at the sky, murmuring. The wind gusts away all syllables before they can be heard. It's the moment before the first letter is inscribed. In this moment we are in București, falling seven storeys onto a page. In a sudden blaze of blue.

Light in the mouth in evening. We both just stay quietly there in our chairs, jubilant on the roof.

—

Later, back in the apartment, I would shut the window and sit down. I would realize the camera was full of photos of E.S. that I had not taken. I'd print them out. I'd know what I had to do. The face, *still,* and the hand. I'd know what I was about to do would ruin translation.

—

I'd bend over the desk and start to write on the back of them.

——

O.: "Books just won't let go of E.'s hands once she gets a grip on them. In the blank space on my bookshelf in București, she left me a note, on the back of a banal photo of two trees rising in a vacant lot beside a building, something like a factory, all windows. My new copy of Derrida's book on mourning: gone. And she's fled. All her note says is: Montreal. Just when I thought I had pinned E.S. down so she could meet E.M., she's absconded. I might as well go back home to Montreal now. There's no use chasing her further."

I shut O.'s notebook after reading this last entry aloud, and hand it back to O. on the roof along with the book on mourning. I've been carrying them around for a while now. I thought I'd startle her for once with my presentation, but there's no startling O. She takes them back with no comment, one hand outstretched to me, not even taking her eyes off the late blue vault of the sky.

I lean back in my chair too and look up. I felt happiness at that moment.

O., if only I could detain time.

PART THREE

Documents for Further Inquiry

—✦✦—

(user please note: from possibly unreliable sources,
prone to viral activity and trojan horses bearing spyware)

E.S. writes to E.M. in the language of no one, regarding the origins of *O Resplandor***:**

I'd seen it first at O.'s house, the one time I was there, a kind of cocktail party in honour of someone and I'd come with someone else, I don't remember who now, just a kind of laugh, fading at my shoulder. For at that point I'd seen it. A photograph enlarged, matted and propped on a table against a wall. In the photo, quite another wall, the outer wall of a building of apartments, one balcony glassed-in in a kind of Galician way. And on the scrub grass, half torn up, that marked the ground, ducks, domestic, at least six of them. So it was the back wall then, and a neighbour's ducks or two neighbours' pecking in the grass, and on this wall, sooted, scratched words, graffitied we might once have said but now inscribed, scripted, the *scri* in that word leaping to the other language, and the ducks — it can't be true — reading the wall.

I entered it first with one shoulder. My arm went into it, my mouth, my ear. Perhaps it was the writing of children, or adolescents — *liviu, liviu,* said the largest of the white writing — perhaps a name that a child might chalk onto a wall, but surely a Galician verb ending and a prefix that said "live" most imperatively to me, that said "book" or *livre, livro,* imperatively. And near this word for book and life, one more word I could distinguish, barely, *frumos.* I knew instantly it was *fermoso* in my own mouth's tongue.

I didn't know O. then. I left without meeting her. I had to go out in the air, the ducks following me. The grass was soaking my shoes. I wasn't lost though. I found my way back around the building and onto Strada Luceafărului.

So whatever else, dear E., it's true we never met, O. and I. Except in the word for *book,* for *beautiful,* for *live.*

From O.'s notebook (appears to be a letter to E.M.):

At last I can describe E.S. to you. How she comes to appear in the
photos. For the book is over. Its title is *O Resplandor*. Really, the
photos are just landscapes, banal like those you meant to take last
year in May in Paris by the bridge where Celan jumped. You took
but four photos there at the Pont Mirabeau, and felt abashed, and
stopped. You wanted to write a love story but you weren't in love,
remember? You wrote on one photo of evening sky, *"tu regardes la
personne que tu étais et tu vois la personne que tu n'as jamais été."*

I can tell you how E.S. comes to appear. There's the photo of a
tramvai and small delivery van passing on a street in Călărași,
and a concrete pole with words scrawled on it — black ink
scuffs, a drawing of a fish upside down, in short, writing — then,
a bit apart from the pole, there's the wind.

Small, this wind. To make it visible (for with wind and writing
both present, visibility is possible), a skirt appears in the space
close to the pole. It *is* not there, there *is* no one in this photo,
but E., when you look at it, you will see a skirt, I know this. The
sewing on a skirt unfurled and making wind visible. Just as a
tree is a scribble made by wind always.

Beside this scribbled skirt (light green like the first leaves of May,
exuding light itself) is a hand now, half hidden, and a hand,
exposed to you.

This is how E.S. enters the photo: for she is made of wind and
writing, and can appear to you between these two. By the time
you see her, her hands have already touched you.

The tram passes to the left. The delivery van heads off to the right and is soon gone. But E.S. Her dark hair catches the wind now. She's looking out of the photo. You can see her knee too, the wind lifts her skirt, there is a pull of thread, and thread, as you know, E., is also writing. E.S. is entirely visible now, a blue bag you'll recognize is slung over her far shoulder; her left shoulder, close to you, utterly bare. Her hair blows across her cheek.

Another tram passes. In its windows are two reflections of blue. The sky. Or you, E.M., about to speak. But when you look up out of this resplendent pool of light, who is it you speak to?

—

(E.M. looks up from her reading of O.'s looped handwriting, and moves her pen to add:)

O. is *writing*. She claims only to translate but she *writes*. With her hands. And the words in her mouth. Her eyes veiled as ever (she said so herself) for their intensity cannot be shown without imperilling the reader.

—

(O.'s last scribble in the notebook is barely legible, and it is not certain what relation it plays to the letter that comes before it.)

Dear E.: Look up. There is no E.S. There is no one in the photos you cannot see when you look up. Yours, O.

A Real Letter
17 xuño 2006, Calgarii, Alberta

Dragă O., I'm so interested in what arises in the present of the
writing moment, in the blurring of the signatures. How this
moment, loosened, immediately undoes or unties the signature. I
feel, once I've written words and assigned them O., O.A., E.M. or
have written across your words and signed them E.S., that I must
give the texts over to you to enact your signature *à travers*, in
whatever way your own present writing moment prompts you:
as commentary, as new lines or liens in your own work. Writing
is thus always already enacted, but moreso. There is continually
a supplement and, like the halo, it is utterly unnecessary and
utterly glowing there. Here. Every enactment or re-enactment of
a signature is a staging, a "making-here" in space.

Yet we each are present as singularities in the text and the texts
we create are at the same time our own, no matter how we sign
them.

Translation, signature. The writing hand, long-fingered and
supple, whose touch remakes an entire interior world.

Today, reading an online Scandinavian litmag of "experimental"
work, I realized that I'm so uninterested in this construct
continually dug up by other people in which "lyric" is split
off and set up against "experiment." I can't even be bothered
to protest it, for protest would just give it credence, in a way. I
am interested in the signature and the mouth and throat. I am
interested in how ear and throat receive language. Which gives
me Bachmann and Beckett fully, which gives me your *rază de
lună* too. And Stănescu.

What's strange to me I guess is how that false dichotomy only looks interesting (perhaps this is it, I am only guessing) from the interior of a monolingualism. Once other languages are part of the foment, the dichotomy does not hold at all; there is but opening, opening. This opening is where we meet as poet-beings. And we get on with our work, which lets us both meet so richly, ever and repeatedly and anew. This "getting on with the work of language" is both lyric, and experiment. Deeply both. Yours, E.

Author photo

Agradecementos e Pensamentos

M.I.M., my mother, who made this book possible, out of impossibility.

Jacques Derrida's *Work on Mourning*, where I learned about friendship, time, gift.

Mirjam Münch, Szymon Kobialka, Roland Steiner, Peter Oelhafen, Anna Wirz-Justice and Christian Cajochen on blue light and circadian rhythms in "Wavelength-dependent Effects of Evening Light Exposure," which E.S. quotes with alterations. Paul Bach-y-Rita, Mitchell E. Tyler and Kurt A. Kaczmarek on activation of the visual cortex by electro-tactile stimulation of the tongue, cited with alterations in O.A.'s notebooks.

Those who thrive with me in the *bouleversement des langues*; Andrés Ajens, Oana Avasilichioaei, Angela Carr, Norma Cole, Chris Daniels, Emeren García, Lani Maestro, Robert Majzels, Belén Martín, Lou Nelson, Chus Pato, María Reimóndez, Elisa Sampedrín, Vida Simon.

Oana Avasilichioaei, a special thanks, for editing the book in September 2009. Also, for her translations of Nichita Stănescu (*Occupational Sickness*) and initial encouragement of Elisa's "translating" that sparked this work in 2006–7. When I appropriated her initials then for the fictive O.A., I had no idea that the real O.A. would return to deftly edit the book.

Hunger Mountain, Chicago Review, Drunken Boat, NO: A Journal of the Arts (all USA); *West Coast Line* (Canada); *Jacket* (Australia); *lemonhound.blogspot.com* (Canada/USA); *Critical Quarterly* (UK); and the limited edition of *12 Elegies from the Romanian of Nichita Stănescu by Elisa Sampedrín*, Montreal: Zat-So Productions, 2007.

I close with two quotes I first read after finishing this book, in that way that reading has of enabling the past as well as the future:

No sé si un libro puede cambiar la vida, pero sí que puede alterar tu reloj biológico. Manuel Rivas, *El País*, 2007.09.08

La poesía es búsqueda de resplandor. Adam Zagajewski, *El País*, 2007.09.22

ERÍN MOURE is the name of one of Canada's most eminent and respected poets, and also a translator from French, Galician, Spanish, and Portuguese. She is the author of thirteen books of poetry, including *Furious*, which won the Governor General's Literary Award; *Domestic Fuel*, which won the Pat Lowther Memorial Award; *Little Theatres*, which won the A.M. Klein Prize for Poetry and was a finalist for the 2006 Griffin Poetry Prize, the Governor General's Literary Award, and the Pat Lowther Memorial Award; *O Cadoiro*, which was a finalist for the A.M. Klein Prize for Poetry and the *ForeWord* Magazine Book of the Year Award; and *Expeditions of a Chimæra* (co-written with Oana Avasilichioaei). Moure has also published seven books of poetry in translation, including *Sheep's Vigil by a Fervent Person* by Alberto Caeiro/Fernando Pessoa, which was a finalist for the 2002 Griffin Poetry Prize and the 2002 City of Toronto Book Prize; Nicole Brossard's *Notebook of Roses and Civilization* (co-translated with Robert Majzels), which was a finalist for the 2008 Griffin Poetry Prize; and Chus Pato's *m-Talá* and *Charenton*. Erín Moure lives in Montreal.